THE FLEET
1840-2004

Designed and produced by

The Open Agency
Mill House
8 Mill Street
London SE1 2BA
www.openagency.com

Written by **Elspeth Wills**

First published 2004
© The Open Agency Limited
Reprinted 2006

All images © Cunard Line except for:
Cover illustration, and pages 130 and 132
by Andrew Davidson. © The Open Agency Limited.
Photograph page 131 © The Open Agency Limited.
Additional images with kind permission from
the Jeff Newman Collection at **www.greatships.net**

ISBN 0-9542451-4-8

Printed in China.

THE FLEET
1840-2004

Cunard's flagships and floating palaces from
the earliest days of steam to Queen Mary 2.

Abstract of Contents.

I. Agreement.

Between

~~The Hon. Mr.~~ Mr Samuel Cunard

on one part

and

Messrs George Burns and David MacIver,

on other part

1. Messrs Burns and MacIver assumed as partners to extent of one half
   in Government Contract for Conveyance of Mails to Halifax
   and in Steam Vessels to be employed

2. Obligation on Mr Cunard to convey to them one half of Government
   Contract
   or to enter along with them into new Contract with Government

3. Obligation on Mr Cunard to grant Power of Attorney to Messrs Burns
   and MacIver to uplift payments from Government

4. Obligation on Messrs Burns and MacIver to pay Mr Cunard Bonus
   of £20,000. for half of Government Contract by Instalments
   at dates specified

CONTENTS

Left The contract of 1839 setting down the
responsibilities of the partners in the new shipping line.

INTRODUCTION

'I want a plain and comfortable boat'

This was the brief that Samuel Cunard issued when he sought a shipbuilder to construct the very first Cunarder. His instructions to his captains were equally direct: 'ship, passengers and mail – bring them safely over and safely back.' One hundred and sixty years and 200 passenger ships later, safety rather than speed, luxury or technology, still comes first.

The history of the Cunard fleet is the story of crossing the North Atlantic, from sail to steam to diesel, from wood to iron to steel. Mail steamers evolved into liners, floating palaces, grand hotels and the holiday resorts of the world's oceans. Some vessels were actors in the great maritime dramas from the rescue of the Titanic to the Battle of the Atlantic. Others left an uneventful wake on the passage of time.

When launching the Queen Mary, Cunard restated its belief in the principles that Samuel had laid down almost a century before. 'A commitment to excellence backed by a long standing reputation for style, comfort and safety ensure that the new Queen will uphold the traditions that have always made Cunard flagships the matriarchs of the ocean.' That commitment holds true in the new Millennium as new Queens accept the ocean's sceptre.

Left Samuel Cunard

CUNARD LINE

BRITISH & NORTH AMERICAN

ROYAL MAIL

STEAM PACKET COMPANY

ESTABLISHED 1840.

THE ATLANTIC STEAMERS
1840-1869

As a boy Samuel Cunard (1787-1865) loved to watch the sailing ships bringing the mail from Europe tie up in the busy port of Halifax, Nova Scotia. When, as a successful middle-aged merchant on a visit to England, he first experienced the speed and efficiency of the new steam engines, it set him dreaming of 'an ocean railway'. In 1838 he happened to read a newspaper advertisement placed by the British Admiralty for a fortnightly Atlantic mail service. Less than three months later, he had won the contract.

In order to achieve his dream Samuel needed ships and money. He found both in Glasgow, the Scottish city on the river Clyde, where entrepreneurial engineer Robert Napier had already made a name for himself as a builder of steam engines for ships. He too had dreamed of an Atlantic steamer service and persuaded Samuel to build a fleet of four ships, larger and more powerful than the Admiralty contract strictly required. Napier introduced Samuel to George and James Burns and David McIver, businessmen experienced in running mail services in British coastal waters. Together they established the British and North American Royal Mail Steam Packet Company. It was not long before the public simply called the new shipping line, Cunard.

Left The cover of the 'Official Guides album to Cunard steamship service' 1878.

When the Britannia swung out of Coburg Dock in Liverpool on 4th July, 1840, one of the world's greatest fleets was born. Her crossing of the Atlantic in a fortnight marked a revolution in communications in an era when mail and newspapers could take six weeks to reach their destination. The little wooden paddle steamer, capable of speeding at nine knots, was soon joined by her sister ships the Acadia, Caledonia and Columbia on the Atlantic run.

The new mail service proved so popular that by 1847 the Admiralty negotiated with Samuel to double the service to sail every Saturday from Liverpool to either Halifax or Boston. The next year Samuel moved the headquarters of his shipping line to London. The contract had laid down that the four new ships should be powerful and capable of carrying guns in time of war. This clause was exercised only seven years later when most of Samuel's fleet was called up for troopship duty during the Crimean War.

The Cunard Atlantic fleet being largely out of action, provided the opportunity for the rival Collins Line, backed by a subsidy from the American Government, to 'proceed with the absolute conquest of this man Cunard' to gain supremacy of the Atlantic. The Collins ships were larger, faster and more luxurious with their bathrooms, barbers' shops, crimson velvet sofas and seashell shaped spittoons for tobacco chewers. Pride, however, came before a fall as Collins sacrificed safety and reliability for speed. A series of tragic accidents at sea bankrupted Collins, leaving him to mourn his wife, son and daughter who went down with one of his ships. Samuel was now 'King of the Atlantic' with a twelve year mail contract in his pocket in return for building even larger ships. By the time of his death in 1865, he had been honoured with a knighthood by Queen Victoria and was master of a fleet that would ensure his immortality.

R.M.S. "BRITANNIA"

1840

'I want a plain but comfortable boat,
not the least unnecessary expense for show.'

Samuel Cunard, 1840.

Above Blueprint for the Britannia. Napier's famous engines
turned her giant paddle wheels on each side of her wooden hull.

BRITANNIA
1840-1880

The Britannia carried 115 first class passengers, 89 crew, 600 tons of coal, the Atlantic mail, chickens, a cow to provide fresh milk and three cats to keep down rats. One passenger summed up her maiden crossing: 'Despite the spartan aspects of the voyage, the saving of time and the reliability of arrival augurs well for steam-propelled trans-Atlantic vessels.'

'She is built long and narrow, and there seems to be a felicitous combination of grandeur, elegance, speed and durability in her construction and material.'

Halifax Recorder, 18th July, 1840.

When the Britannia was iced up in Boston Harbor in 1844, the city's merchants organised a team of lumberjacks and labourers to plough a seven mile channel to the open sea. Half the population skated alongside as the Britannia slowly made her way through the ice. Concerned that Cunard might desert Boston for New York, the merchants waived the bill. Cunard remained faithful to the city for many years, despite launching an additional New York sailing in 1847.

CALEDONIA
1840-1851

With her characteristic red and black funnel, the Caledonia was one of Britannia's three sisters. Like all early Cunarders she carried a full set of sails in case her engines broke down in mid-Atlantic. Fearing fires and explosions, many travellers were reluctant to cross on one of the new-fangled steamships which the clergy denounced from the pulpit as 'the work of the Devil'.

HALIFAX AND BOSTON
ROYAL MAIL.

THE **HIBERNIA** starts on **WEDNESDAY,** the
h of October.—*At Three o'Clock,* on the
fternoon of that day, a Steamer will be at
e Egremont Slip, south end of the Prince's
ock, to take off the Passengers.

☞ Passengers are particularly requested to
ad all Luggage on board the day before. *George*

h Ferry Steamer Every Hour

BILL OF FARE

STEAM SHIP HIBERNIA.

17 **day of** *October 1843.*

BREAKFAST.

Dishes of Beef Steaks.
- Do.   Mutton Chops.
- Do.   Pork Chops.
- Do.   Veal Cutlets.
- Do.   Smoked Salmon.
- Do.   Broiled Chicken.
- Do.   Fried Ham.
- Do.   Cold Meats.
- Do.   Stews.

Eggs in Omelettes.
- Do.   Boiled.

Hominy.
Mush.

DINNER.

	ROAST.	BOILED.
Soup Beef Turkey		
Dishes Fish		
2 Do. Beef		
2 Do. Mutton		
Do. Lamb		
1 Do. Veal		

HIBERNIA
1843-1868

Like her sister the Cambria, the
Hibernia was slightly larger and
more powerful than the first four
Cunarders. Although Samuel
cautioned his captains to put
safety before speed at all costs,
the Hibernia broke the eastbound
Atlantic record in the year of her
maiden voyage while two years
later the even faster Cambria
made the westbound crossing in
under ten days.

Left For the first few days out of port,
passengers on the Hibernia enjoyed smoked
salmon or mutton chops for breakfast and
calves' cheeks and strawberry tart for dinner.
In mid-Atlantic the fare was simpler as ships
relied heavily on dried goods in the days
before refrigeration. Vegetables were kept
fresh by storing them under the lifeboats.

EUROPA
1848-1867

'Once a week comes a Cunard steamer, with its red funnel
pipe whitened by the salt spray and firing off cannon to
announce her arrival. For several hours afterwards she lies
with the smoke and steam coming out of her, as if she
were smoking her pipe after her toilsome passage across
the Atlantic.'

Nathaniel Hawthorne, author and US consul in Liverpool, 1853.

With cheaper postage, letters were soon dashing across the Atlantic.
In 1847 Samuel commissioned the America, the Canada, the Europa
and the Niagara to meet demand and fulfil his side of the new
Admiralty mail contract.

They were the first ships to use navigation lights at night - port red,
starboard green, and foremasthead white. Despite this the Europa was
somewhat accident prone. In 1849 she collided with the US emigrant
ship, Charles Bartlett, which sank with the loss of 135 lives. Nine years
later she collided with fellow Cunarder, the Arabia, off Newfoundland
although both managed to limp into port.

ASIA
1850-1876

Although twice the tonnage of Britannia, the Asia and her sister the Africa were outclassed by the new Collins Line ships.

'A steamer of the Collins Line,
A Yankee Doodle Notion,
Has also quickest cut the brine
Across the Atlantic Ocean,
And British agents, no way slow
Her merits to discover,
Have been and bought her just to tow –
The Cunard packets over.'

Contemporary satire from **Punch magazine,** *1852.*

ARABIA
1853-1868

The Arabia welcomed several new types of passenger on board. For the first time, young children had their own nursery while troops marched on deck during the Crimean War. She also carried over the 7,500 cavalry horses that saw active service in the Crimea, slung in canvas hammocks on her decks. After the disastrous Charge of the Light Brigade, her return load was much lighter. In 1861 she became the first Cunarder to carry royalty, when Prince Alfred, Queen Victoria's second son, returned from visiting Canada.

PERSIA
1856-1872

Cunard rose to the Collins Line challenge. When launched in 1855, the iron-hulled Persia was the largest ship afloat. On her maiden voyage she gave her rival the Pacific a three day head start in the race to be first across. Late and badly damaged from hitting an iceberg, the Persia limped into New York Harbor expecting to find a jubilant Collins Line ship. The Pacific, with over 180 passengers on board, was not at her moorings: she had disappeared without trace in mid-Atlantic. Until 1870 the Persia and the Scotia reigned supreme as Blue Riband holders.

Left Launch of the Persia, Glasgow, 1855.

SCOTIA
1862-1904

The Scotia, Cunard's last paddle steamer, was much admired.

'*Stupendous as the Scotia is, the lines of beauty have been so well worked out in the preparation of her model that her appearance is singularly graceful. This mighty fabric, so beautiful as a whole, is made up of innumerable pieces of ponderous metal, welded, jointed, and riveted into each other with exceeding deftness.*'

Glasgow Herald, 1862.

CHINA
1862-1906

Cunard was conservative about adopting new technology. With the China and the Scotia, the shipping line compared the merits of screw propellers over paddle wheels. The bare-sided China proving more efficient and economical, screw propulsion was here to stay. Cunard was also slow to enter the emigrant business, the China being its first vessel to carry significant numbers of steerage passengers.

RUSSIA
1867-1902

'We encountered a heavy NW gale with tremendous billows. The Russia took it all with ease, and towered up one wave and down the bottom of another in the most elegant manner.'

Liverpool business traveller on the Russia, 1872.

On his second US tour, author Charles Dickens travelled home on the Russia. He was full of praise for the ship, from his commodious cabin to the fragrance of the flowers in the passenger saloon. It was a very different experience from his voyage on the Britannia in 1842 when he described the saloon as being *'not unlike a gigantic hearse with windows'* and his bunk as *'a thin mattress, spread like a surgical plaster on a most inaccessible shelf'*.

Left Dickens's cabin on the Russia.
Right Painting of the Russia which once hung in Cunard's London office.

EMIGRANT SHIPS TO LUXURY LINERS
1870-1899

In one of the greatest movements of people in history, over 11 million emigrants crossed the Atlantic between 1860 and 1900, some to escape poverty and persecution and others to seek adventure or a better way of life. The Californian Gold Rush and the Canadian Government's offer of an assisted passage and free land to populate the prairies swelled the numbers. About a third of the emigrants sailed from Liverpool, Cunard's home port.

Cunard had been slow to enter the emigrant market, the China (1862) being its first ship with steerage accommodation. New shipping lines like Inman and White Star were already growing rich on this business. In 1870 White Star also challenged Cunard on its home ground with the Oceanic, the ship that took trans-Atlantic steamers into the 'travelling palace class'. The Oceanic had undreamed of luxuries: there were spacious staterooms served by stewards who could be summoned at the press of an ivory button, and lavatories close by to replace the nightly chamber pot. From set menus to iced water, the newer shipping lines also treated their steerage passengers with increasing respect.

In the 1870s Cunard was losing money and momentum, its board resistant to these new 'frivolities'. They saw no reason to move away from Samuel's 'plain and comfortable boats'. A financial crisis in 1878 forced through change, symbolised by the new house flag emblazoned with the proud lion holding a globe that still flies on Cunarders today. The new chairman, John Burns, ushered in an era of renewed vigour and growth with eight new ships on the high seas by 1885: 'the Company which reduces the time in crossing the Atlantic will ensure success in the long run … I have faith in the future, a confidence that the Cunard Company will hold its own on the Atlantic.' Under his helmsmanship Cunard was to be the only major British shipping line on the Atlantic to survive into the 20th century.

Although they still carried sails for emergencies Cunarders like the Umbria (1884) and the Etruria (1885) were beginning to look like liners rather than steamships. They were record breakers in more than speed: the impact of their new-fangled refrigeration chambers was immediately felt on the menu. In 1884 Cunard also built the vessel that was to carry the shipping line's greatest number of passengers ever: this was the tender Skirmisher which ferried passengers to the liners until 1945.

By the mid 1890s Cunard had a fleet to be proud of. With steel hulls and reliable propulsion, its ships adopted the best of proven technology, regularly capturing the Blue Riband. The first, twin-screw sisters, Campania (1893) and Lucania (1893), represented not only a new generation of speed but of luxury. Gentlemen lounged on the velvet ottomans or swivelled on revolving chairs to eavesdrop on a neighbouring dinner table conversation. The ladies' room was even perfumed by fresh geraniums.

There was one portent of challenging times ahead. In 1897 the Norddeutscher Lloyd Line's Kaiser Wilhelm der Grosse set off on her maiden voyage. She was the largest and longest liner afloat; her interiors were the last word in opulence and she was the first liner to boast four funnels. That year, for the first time, the Blue Riband was in German hands.

PARTHIA

1870-1956

With accommodation for over a thousand third class passengers, the long-lived Parthia was very much an emigrant ship. Compound engines meant that she required half the amount of coal to maintain the same speed as her sister ships, the Abyssinia and the Algeria. With less coal, there was more space on deck for emigrants to enjoy a chat or contemplate their new life. Passengers could also wash away the smuts from her funnel as the Parthia was the first Cunarder to have baths, one on the port side and one on the starboard.

BATAVIA
1870-1924

American author Mark Twain was a passenger on the Batavia in 1872. It was an unusually exciting voyage as the Cunarder went to the rescue of a stricken sailing ship in near hurricane conditions. 'To a landsman it seemed like deliberate suicide to go out in such a storm, but our third and fourth officers and eight men answered the call with a promptness that compelled a cheer.'

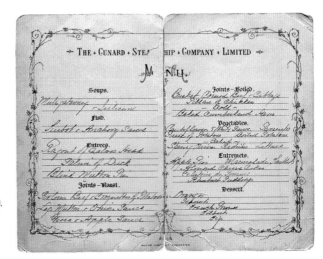

Right By 1882 headings on Cunard menus were printed, although the chef still wrote in the names of the dishes, from mulligatawny soup to rhubarb pudding, in immaculate copperplate.

BOTHNIA

1874-1899

Above This trade card of around 1880 extolled the virtues of the Bothnia's covered-in promenade deck. Cabins and saloons no longer risked being swamped in 'boisterous' weather.

The Bothnia and her sister the Scythia (1875) each accommodated over 1,100 steerage passengers. Henry Knight, a privileged first class passenger went exploring in 1881: 'the cabins are good with two tiers of beds each side and a passage down the middle, each shelf of beds holding five or six persons, women on one side men on the other — married people and families having separate cabins — many of them are very dirty and all seem very poor.'

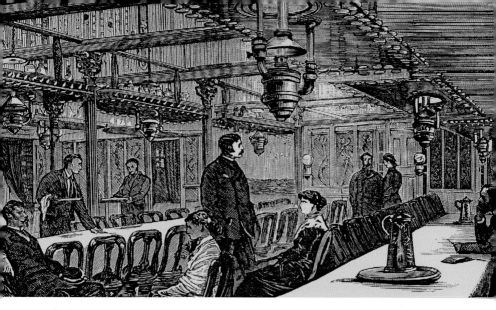

GALLIA
1879-1900

First class passengers still dined at long tables which doubled up as the cocktail bar. Travel enthusiast Mark Twain sailed on the Gallia in her maiden year. In an interview with the New York Times he praised the ship's stability but, even when pressed, was not prepared 'to say whether a cocktail, left standing on his cabin's shelf at night, would be there all safe in the morning.'

Left The Gallia was the last Cunarder not strictly entitled to the name as, like her predecessors, she was commissioned by Samuel's original company, the British & North American Steamship Navigation Co.

CATALONIA
1881-1901

The Catalonia, the first true Cunarder, was a sturdy if slow emigrant ship with ample space for cargo as well as passengers. The year after her maiden voyage, Irish-born Thomas Moriarty had a less than happy end to his home-coming from Boston when customs officers discovered smuggled tobacco, an unlicensed revolver and 100 rounds of ammunition in his luggage.

During her career, the Catalonia was twice requisitioned to deliver troops to the scene of action, in Egypt in 1882 and South Africa in 1899.

Left Ticket receipt for a voyage on Cunard Line's Catalonia, 1881.

PAVONIA
1882-1900

Sister to the Catalonia and the Cephalonia, the Pavonia was not one of Cunard's more reliable ships. In 1892 her propeller snapped in mid-Atlantic and she had to be towed to Boston by a German steamship. Seven years later, despite her three masts being fully equipped with sails, she was under tow again, this time from the Azores to Liverpool. The next year she was scrapped.

Left With 1,500 steerage passengers on board, the select 200 who travelled 'saloon class' liked to be reassured that they were in good company. Passenger lists like this which also highlighted the route were carefully checked to spot acquaintances and social climbers.

SERVIA
1881-1902

The Servia was a first class ship and the second largest on the ocean. She was the first Cunarder to be built of steel and could speed along at 16 knots. Boasting electric light and the largest staircase at sea, her interior even impressed royal visitors accustomed to palaces. 'The Times' noted: 'It is almost needless to say that his Royal Highness expressed great pleasure with all he saw, and he was particularly struck with the spaciousness and luxury of the arrangements in the successive tiers of berths which rise one above another like the storeys of a house.'

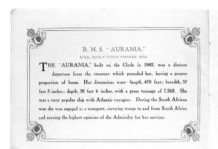

AURANIA
1883-1905

The Aurania was a big beamed ship, her extra girth making her more stable in rough seas. Her breadth was an eighth of her length whereas that of her predecessors was usually a tenth. Although she carried emigrants, she also offered new luxuries for first class passengers from suites of cabins to marble bathrooms. She inaugurated a number of new services including the first mid-week sailings from Liverpool to New York and the first Trieste-New York run for emigrants, thousands of whom were Jews fleeing persecution in Eastern Europe.

Above The Aurania featured in this beautifully illustrated history of Cunard published in the 1930s.

UMBRIA
1884-1910

ETRURIA
1885-1910

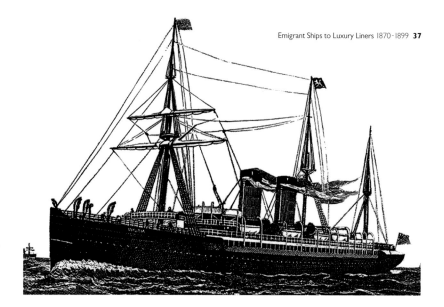

With their tall funnels and solid superstructure, sister ships Umbria and Etruria were the first Cunarders to look like modern liners. They were also the last to carry sail. With their three powerful compound engines, they raced each other for the Blue Riband. In 1903 the Umbria narrowly escaped disaster, when the New York police were tipped off that a bomb was on the steamer pier waiting to be loaded. The 100lbs of explosive were safely defused and fingers pointed at the Mafia.

The ship's cat had good reason to lick its lips. On a single Atlantic voyage in 1886 the Etruria was stocked with '12,550lbs fresh beef, 760lbs corned beef, 5,320lbs mutton, 850lbs lamb, 350lbs veal, 350lbs pork, 2,000lbs fresh fish, 600 fowls, 300 chickens, 100 ducks, 50 geese, 80 turkeys, 200 brace grouse, 220 quarts of ice cream, 1,000 quarts of milk and 11,500 eggs'. One egg could be consumed every minute all the way from Liverpool to New York.

CAMPANIA
1893-1918

LUCANIA
1893-1909

Atlantic greyhounds Campania and Lucania, the first Cunarders to have twin screw propellers, were built for speed. Their funnels were raked backwards to enhance the impression of motion while their bows were almost unraked, slicing the water like a knife. The bridge was high up towards the bow to give the helmsman a clear view and the redundant masts became flagpoles.

Cunard's investment paid off. In 1893 the Campania became the first Cunarder to cross in under six days, winning the Blue Riband for her performance. The two ships remained neck and neck until in 1897 the Lucania came close to breaking the 5 day barrier.

Right Contemporary newspaper advertisement for the two liners 'The Largest, Fastest and Most Magnificent in the World.'

WHEN SENDING FOR YOUR FRIENDS
Secure Passage by the Old Reliable
CUNARD MAIL LINE
which has been in existence
over 56 Years, and Never Lost a Passenger's Life
and has made the Fastest Time on Record
5 DAYS 7 Hours 23 Minutes.
The New Twin-Screw Steamships,
LUCANIA AND CAMPANIA
620 ft. Long, 12,950 Tons, 30,000 H.-P.
The Largest, Fastest and Most Magnificent
in the World.
UMBRIA, ETRURIA, AURANIA, SERVIA,
520 ft. Long, 8500 Tons, 14,500 Horse-power.
and other Floating Palaces, comprising an incomparable fleet of Fast-Express Passenger Steamers.
Saturday Sailings from New York, Boston and Liverpool, calling at Queenstown.
Unequalled Second-Cabin and Steerage accommodation on all steamers.
F. G. WHITING, Mgr. Clark and Randolph. Chicago.
GRAHAM & SONS, 134 W. Madison St., Chicago.

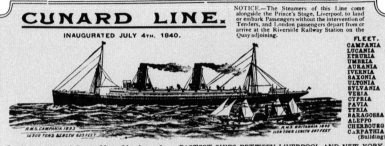

Above 'Fastest ships . . . unsurpassed accommodation.'
Superlatives were beginning to slip into Cunard advertising.

Even in old age the Campania was a record breaker. After 250 crossings she was nearing her final journey to the scrap yard when the First World War broke out. Winning a new lease of life as a seaplane carrier, she made naval history in April 1915 as the first ship to launch an aircraft whilst underway.

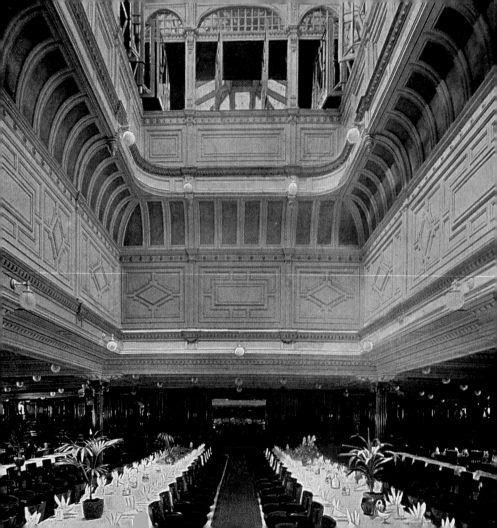

The Campania and the Lucania were designed to make first class passengers feel that they were at home with the aristocracy. The Lucania was the first Cunarder to offer single berth cabins and her stateroom suites were sought after by millionaires.

These 'wonder ships' boasted some of the most sumptuous interiors yet seen on the Atlantic. Their first class drawing rooms were 60ft long and 30ft wide. The walls were of satinwood with cedar mouldings and the ceilings were enriched with old ivory and gilt. Furnishings included Persian carpets, brocade settees and velvet drapes. Here passengers could while away the time with the latest novel from the ship's library or enjoy a recital on the grand piano or the American organ.

In the dining room, lit dramatically from above, from 1901 passengers could find the first daily newspaper at sea lying beside their napkins thanks to Mr Marconi's wireless telegraph. Gentlemen checked their stocks against Wall Street while their wives caught up with the latest society gossip. Passengers were soon in touch with the technology: finding himself out of pocket, H. Robertson, a first class passenger on the Campania, cabled his mother to arrange for money to be ready for his arrival in New York.

Far left Cunard was so proud of its 430 seater first class dining room that it put a lion on the back of every seat.
Left Campania at sea.

'The smoking room with its coach roof and piazzala arrangement of chairs along the sides, had the air of a cathedral choir, slightly cheered by the brassy glow of an open fire grate, a hearth shiny with Persian tiles, an Oriental rug in front of it. The whole tone of the room was suggestive of 'otium cum digniate'.'

Left Cunard published a 108 page brochure to extol the interior fittings of the Campania and the Lucania which it summed up as 'a silent sermon in good taste.' In the brochure only one sentence was devoted to steerage which was 'in every way excellent'.

THE ELEGANT EDWARDIANS
1900-1914

By 1900 passengers were demanding ever greater comfort and speed. The emigrant trade was booming while growing numbers of Americans had the time and money to summer in Europe. The wealthy expected their liners to emulate the luxury and style of an English country house or the best Riviera hotel. Below decks, third class offering basic amenities like clean sheets, public lounges and a choice of menu was rapidly replacing steerage. Second generation emigrants returning to visit their families were joined here by a new breed of young, adventurous Americans eager to 'do Europe'.

Cunard responded by replacing its ageing fleet with fast modern liners and by extending its services from European ports to serve the growing emigrant trade from Eastern Europe. It gradually adopted the new technology of steam turbine engines, giving greater speed, efficiency and a smoother ride for passengers. The interiors of its 'floating palaces' surpassed even Edwardian expectations of opulence as well as boasting new facilities like gyms and shopping arcades. As Cunard boasted of the Aquitania, ocean travel was now 'the thing': 'Half the pleasure of doing a thing really well consists of letting the other people - the ones who are not doing the thing at all, but would like to if they could - know that one is enjoying the very best that there is to be had.'

The highly charged international atmosphere, that was to erupt into 'the war to end all wars' in 1914, extended to the Altantic where competition, especially between Britain and Germany, was intense. Winning the Blue Riband or building the largest liner became a symbol of national pride. When US billionaire John Pierpont Morgan bought Liverpool's White Star Line in 1902 to fulfil his ambition to own the North Atlantic, Britain trembled at this audacious threat to her supremacy of the seas.

In 1903 the British Government retaliated by giving financial backing to Cunard to build two superliners - the Mauretania and the Lusitania - provided they were designed to be the fastest ships on the Atlantic and capable of conversion into armed cruisers in the event of war. These 'Monarchs of the Sea' not only brought the Blue Riband back to Britain but won hands down in elegance against the heavy ornateness of the German liners and the brashness of their American equivalents. Tragedy unwittingly reinforced Cunard's victory in 1912 when White Star's Titanic sank after colliding with an iceberg on her maiden voyage. The Cunard emigrant ship Carpathia plucked 703 survivors from the Titanic's lifeboats, adrift in the ice-strewn sea. J. P. Morgan was rarely seen in public again.

An even grander sister ship, the Aquitania was launched from the Clyde on 21st April, 1913 in front of a cheering crowd of 100,000 and amid a blaze of publicity. Not only was she to be the largest liner in the world but also the most sumptuous vessel on the North Atlantic. Future passengers were also reassured that there would be space on a lifeboat for everyone. The Aquitania's maiden voyage, however, on 30th May, 1914 was overshadowed by the sinking of the Empress of Ireland, when she collided with a collier in dense fog, with the loss of 1,012 lives. World events were soon to cast an even greater shadow as, after only three crossings, the Aquitania was requisitioned for war, along with many of the Cunard fleet.

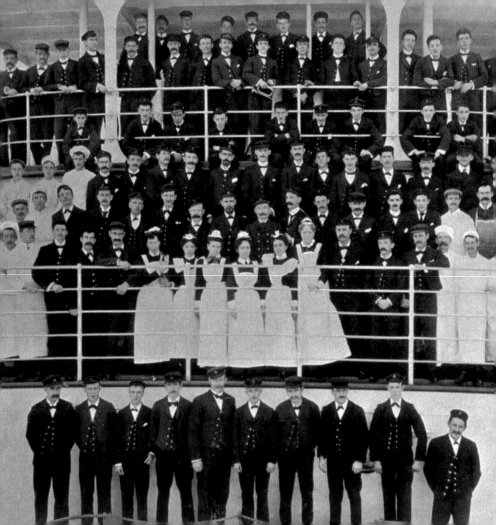

IVERNIA
1900-1916

SAXONIA
1900-1925

'The Ivernia and the Saxonia were big, solid, reliable ships. When launched the Ivernia was the largest cargo vessel afloat as well as having basic accommodation for 1,600 third class passengers.

Especially in an era when funnels were fashionable, the sister ships were unusual in having only one, albeit gigantic, smokestack. There was no mistaking the Saxonia as she came over the horizon as her funnel was the tallest in the world, a staggering 106 ft from deck to cowl.

Opposite The crew of the Saxonia line up on deck.

CARPATHIA
1903-1918

A near sister to the Ivernia and the Saxonia, the Carpathia had an uneventful career as an emigrant ship until 14th April, 1912 when her radio officer Harold Cottam received the message that was to make her a legend: 'We have struck ice. Come at once.' The Carpathia's Captain Rostron laconically described what happened next: 'We steamed at full speed and did what we could.' She dashed to the last known position of the Titanic at over three knots more than her normal speed of 14 knots. When she arrived, there was no trace of the 'titanic Titanic', the ship that claimed to be unsinkable. On 17th July, 1918, while still in service as a passenger liner, the Carpathia joined the Titanic in the graveyard of the Atlantic, after being struck by three torpedoes from a German U-boat.

TITANIC SINKS FOUR HOURS AFTER HITTING ICEBERG; 866 RESCUED BY CARPATHIA, PROBABLY 1250 PERISH; ISMAY SAFE, MRS. ASTOR MAYBE, NOTED NAMES MISSING

**ol. Astor and Bride,
sidor Straus and Wife,
and Maj. Butt Aboard.**

RULE OF SEA" FOLLOWED

omen and Children Put Over
Lifeboats and Are Supposed
to be Safe on Carpathia.

PICKED UP AFTER 8 HOURS

ncent Astor Calls at White Star
Office for News of His Father
and Leaves Weeping.

FRANKLIN HOPEFUL ALL DAY

nager of the Line Insisted
tanic Was Unsinkable Even
After She Had Gone Down.

HEAD OF THE LINE ABOARD

Bruce Ismay Making First Trip on
Gigantic Ship That Was to
Surpass All Others.

The Lost Titanic Being Towed Out of Belfast Harbor.

Biggest Liner Plunges to the Bottom at 2:20 A. M.

RESCUERS THERE TOO LATE

Except to Pick Up the Few Hundreds Who Took to the Lifeboats.

WOMEN AND CHILDREN FIRST

Cunarder Carpathia Rushing to New York with the Survivors.

SEA SEARCH FOR OTHERS

The California Stands By on Chance of Picking Up Other Boats or Rafts.

OLYMPIC SENDS THE NEWS

Only Ship to Flash Wireless Messages to Shore After the Disaster.

LATER REPORT SAVES 866.

BOSTON, April 15.—A wireless message picked up late to-night, relayed from the Olympic, says that the Carpathia is on her way to New York with 866 passengers from the steamer Titanic aboard. They are mostly women and children, the message said, and it concluded: "Grave fears are felt for the safety of the balance of the passengers and crew."

Special to The New York Times.

CAPE RACE, N. F., April 15.—The White Star liner Olympic reports by wireless this evening that the Cunarder Carpathia reached, at daybreak this morning, the position from which wireless calls for help were sent out last night by the Titanic after her collision with an iceberg. The Carpathia found only the lifeboats and the wreckage of what had been the biggest steamship afloat.

The Titanic had foundered at about 2:20 A. M., in latitude 41:16 north and longitude 50:14 west. This is about 30 minutes

PARTIAL LIST OF THE SAVED.

Includes Bruce Ismay, Mrs. Widener, Mrs. H. B. Harris, and an incomplete name, suggesting Mrs. Astor's.

Special to The New York Times.

CAPE RACE, N. F., Tuesday, April 16.—Following is a partial list of survivors among the first-class passengers of the Titanic, received by the Marconi wireless station this morning from the Carpathia, via the steamship Olympic:

Mrs. JACOB P.	and maid.	Mr. C. ROLMANE.	Mrs. WILLIAM BUCKNELL.
Mr. HARRY ANDERSON.	Mrs. SUSAN P. ROGERSON. (Probably Rycrson.)	Mrs. O. M. BARKWORTH.
Mr. ED. W. APPLETON.	Mrs. ARTHUR ROGERSON.	Mrs. H. B. STEFFASON.
Mrs. ROSE ABBOTT.	Master ALLISON and nurse.	Mrs. ELSIE BOWERMAN.
Miss G. M. BURNS.	Miss E. T. ANDREWS.	
Miss D. D. CASSEBENE.	Miss NINETTE PANHART.	The Marconi station reports that it relayed the word after "Mrs. Jacob P." It is first received by the Associated Press this morning this name appeared well down, but in Two Times it is placed first, suggesting that the name of the first John Jacob Astor is intended. This supposition is strengthened by the fact that Mrs. H. J. Allison Mrs. Astor is the only lady to the "A" column of this passenger list attended by a maid.
Mrs. WM. M. CLARKE.	Miss E. W. ALLEN.	
Mrs. E. CHIBNACE.	Mr. and Mrs. D. BISHOP.	
Mr. H. E. CROSBIE.	Mr. H. BLANK.	
Mr. ROSKOU.	Mrs. A. BARRIVA.	
Miss JEAN HIFACE.	Mrs. JAMES BAXTER.	
Mr. HY. B. HARRIS.	Mr. GEORGE A. NATT.	
Mrs. ALEX. HALVERSON.	Miss C. POWELL.	
Miss MARGARET BAYE.	Mr. J. M. BROWN.	
Mr. BRUCE ISMAY.	Mr. G. T. BOWEN.	
Mr. and Mrs. ED. KIMBERLEY.	Mr. and Mrs. R. L. BECKY	NAMES PICKED UP AT BOSTON.
Mr. J. A. MENTMAN.	Miss RUTH TAUSSIG.	BOSTON, April 15.—Among the
Mrs. EMILE KENCHEN.	Miss ELLA THOR	
Mr. G. F. LONGLEY.		
Mr. A.F LEADER.		

Special to The New York Times.

CAPE RACE, N. F., April 15.

admitting that the Titanic, the
gest steamship in the world, had
n sunk by an iceberg and had gone
the bottom of the Atlantic, probably
rrying more than 1,800 of her pas-
gers and crew with her, was made
the White Star Line offices, it
esday, at 8:20 o'clock last night,
Mr. P. A. S. Franklin, Vice Presi-
t General Manager of the Interna-
al Mercantile Marine, conceded that
obably only those passengers who
ad picked up by the Cunarder Car-
thia had been saved. Advices re-
ed early this morning tended to
rease the number of survivors by

The admission followed a day in
ich the White Star Line officials
d been optimistic in the extreme. At
time was the admission made that
ey conceded the huge steamer was
a safe. The ship itself, it was confi-
ntly asserted, was unsinkable, and
wers were informed that she would
be kept, under her own steam prob-
ly, but surely with the help of the
New York Virginian, which was re-
rted to be towing her.

As the day passed, however, with no
authentic reports from the Titanic
any of the ships which were known
have responded to her wireless call
help, it became apparent that un-

CARONIA
1905-1933

Above The Caronia stretches along Fifth Avenue

The Carmania and the Caronia ushered in the era of the high-sided steamer, their languid elegance leading admirers to call them the 'pretty sisters'. Cunard was so proud of its new liners that it compared them with the world's great landmarks. Comparisons between the 'pretty sisters' extended below the waterline. The superior performance of the Carmania, the first Cunarder fitted with turbines, against the Caronia with her conventional quadruple expansion engines convinced the shipping line to adopt the new turbine technology for its planned super-liners, Mauretania and Lusitania.

The funnels of the 'pretty sisters' wore a new livery. Traditionally funnels had been painted in five equal parts, one fifth black and the other four fifths Cunard red. The proportions of these vessels dictated the change to a quarter black and three quarters red.

CARMANIA
1905-1931

Many of the 1.8m immigrants to Canada between 1891 and 1911 travelled Cunard. Although still strictly confined to their own quarters, the Caronia's 2,000 third class passengers enjoyed reasonable standards of accommodation. While third class ladies could retire to their own sitting area, first class ladies enjoyed the novelty of joining the gentlemen for coffee and brandy after dinner in the newly introduced lounge.

LUSITANIA
1907-1915

MAURETANIA
1907-1935

Right Cunard produced an
illustrated booklet to impress
upon the eager public the
incredible size of the liners
and the feats of engineering
involved in their building.

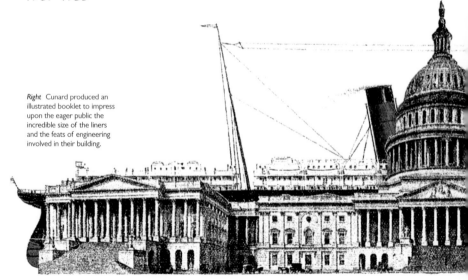

" LUSITANIA " AND " MAURETANIA

The Mauretania (1907) and the Lusitania (1907) were true 'Monarchs of the Sea', designed to outclass the German monster liners like Kaiser Wilhelm der Grosse and the Deutschland. Cunard decreed that their accommodation was to be 'of a spaciousness and splendour hitherto unknown outside the great luxury hotels of the world'.

First class passengers could adopt an aristocratic pose in public rooms modelled on English country houses and French chateaux. Even the bath taps in their cabins were silver plated. Their names had an extra syllable for added dignity. Unfamiliar with these titles of Roman provinces, the public soon affectionately called the liners 'Maury' and 'Lucy'.

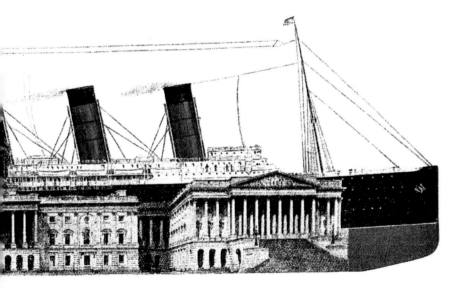

ND THE CAPITOL, WASHINGTON.

A GAME of WHIST in a PRIVATE SITTING ROOM.

IN THE GENERAL DRAWING ROOM

LUNCHEON in the GRAND SALOON

Views of the CUNARD Express Turbine Steamers "LU

EARLY MORNING COFFEE & THE NEWSPAPER IN THE OPEN AIR CAFE

'ANIA" AND "MAURETANIA."

Dining was a more sumptuous experience for all classes on the Mauretania and Lusitania. In the Mauretania's French Renaissance first class dining room, electric lamps, concealed in the gold dome, cast a soft glow over diners while both ships celebrated their technological modernity with Express Turbine restaurants. Even third class passengers enjoyed clean table cloths and waiter service as well as a piano for volunteer musicians.

'Words fail to convey any adequate idea of the beauty of the public rooms, the chaste perfection of the decorative schemes, the all-pervading sense of spaciousness, and the general excellence both of material and workmanship'.

Cunard Daily Bulletin, Fashion and Pleasure Resort Supplement, 1907.

The sisters were designed to be the fastest ships on the Atlantic. The Lusitania snatched the Blue Riband from the German Deutschland on her second outward voyage, crossing to New York in 4 days 19 hours and 52 minutes. The Mauretania proved her staying power. Although fog prevented her from winning the Blue Riband on her maiden voyage, she claimed the first of her eight eastbound records on the return leg. Two years later 'the Queen of the Blue Riband' snatched the westbound record from her sister, retaining the title until 1929.

They had also been built for war as well as peace. As a condition of Government support towards their construction in 1903, they had to be capable of carrying guns and of travelling at 25 knots in order to outpace submarines. All their vital organs from engines to boilers were placed below the waterline for safety, as was the practice in warship design.

The Mauretania was called up on the outbreak of the First World War in 1914. She served as a troop ship in the Mediterranean, her speed allowing her to escape a U-boat attack. She carried North American troops to Europe and, with the Aquitania, brought 130,000 triumphantly back in 1918.

Above Winning the Blue Riband was good for business. Cunard posters regularly advertised the sailings of the fastest ocean liners in the world.
Opposite Motor vehicles were starting to join the horses, carts and carriages on the quayside when a great liner docked.

She went on to enjoy many years of crossing and increasingly of cruising before being retired in 1935.

The Lusitania had a tragic fate. While still serving as a passenger liner, she left New York for Liverpool on 1st May, 1915, with 1,959 passengers and crew on board. The busy sea lanes off the Irish coast were rich hunting grounds for German U-boats and U-20 spotted the four funnels of a big kill. The Lusitania took only 18 minutes to sink with the loss of over 1,200 lives. Passenger A.B. Cross recalled his experience: 'Then came the worst part. We were alone. The space a few moments ago occupied by our luxurious home was a ghastly blank of almost still water.'

ALBANIA
(1911-1930)

ASCANIA
(1911-1918)

AUSONIA
(1911-1918)

With Canada encouraging settlers to its empty prairies, in 1911 Cunard acquired three ships from the Thomson Line - the Albania, the Ascania and the Ausonia - for a new Southampton-Montreal service. This was the first time that Cunard sailed from what is now its home port of Southampton and that its ships made their way up the St Lawrence when not blocked by ice.

Right The Ascania heralded the start of a new life.

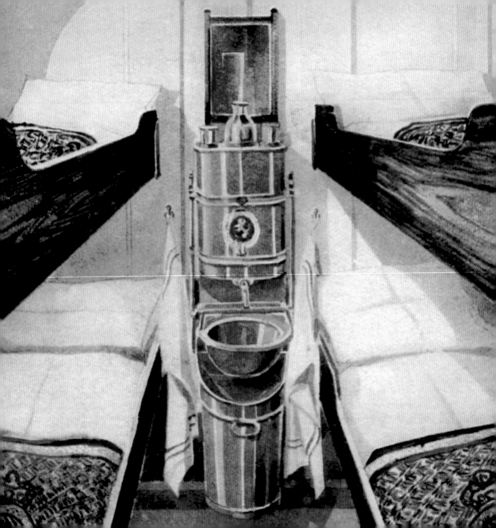

ANDANIA
1913-1918

ALAUNIA
1913-1916

AURANIA II
1917-1918

In 1913 Cunard decided that it needed its own custom-designed ships for the new Canadian route, ordering the Andania, Alaunia and Aurania from the Clyde. The ships were almost identical, with only second and third class accommodation. The crew to passenger ratio was much lower than on the 'floating hotels' with around 290 crew to look after over 2,000 travellers and their ship. Four and six berth cabins replaced the traditional dormitories of steerage.

None of the trio survived the First World War, the Andania and the Aurania falling victim to torpedo attacks and the Alaunia being mined in the English Channel.

Opposite By now, the basic amenities were all too close for comfort in this 3rd class cabin on the Andania.

AQUITANIA
1914-1949

The Aquitania was the greatest four funnelled Cunarder of all, her interiors the marvel of the North Atlantic. Her public rooms captured the style of different eras from her smoking room modelled on Greenwich Hospital to her elegant, Adam-style first class drawing room decorated with prints of ports and royalty.

Her lavish public rooms were the setting for entertainments from masked balls in the verandah gardens to impromptu performances by theatre companies rehearsing their next Broadway or West End success.

In the 1920s gamblers could while away the time by taking on a retired card sharper at whist or by betting on the number of miles the liner had travelled in the last 24 hours. The socially aspiring could jostle for an invitation to the lavish table of Captain Sir Charles James whose gargantuan appetite matched his waistline.

Left Skyscrapers increasingly dominated the New York skyline.
Opposite A man may look at a gigantic rudder. This one steered the Aquitania, the longest surviving Cunarder of the 20th century, safely through two World Wars and thousands of miles of wild and empty ocean.

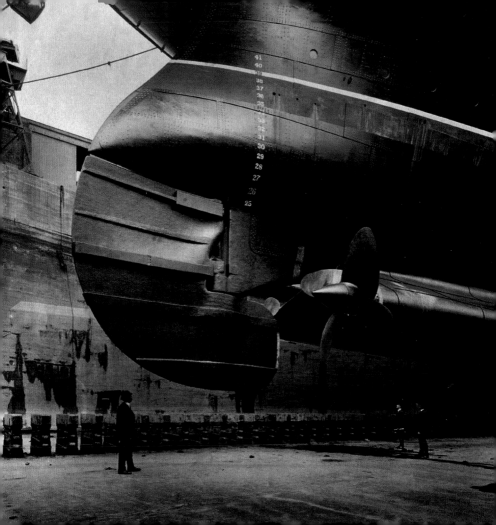

Above The Aquitania had only completed three crossings when war broke out. Five thousand men were employed to remove her finery. Two thousand wagon loads of everything from painted cornices to Chippendale tables were removed from the two liners in 48 hours for storage in warehouses around Liverpool. *Right* Only three years after the interior decorators moved out, a team of artists moved in to givie the Aquitania a coat of dazzle paint. This helped to confuse German U-boats as she plied the North Atlantic laden with troops after America's entry into the First World War.

THE ONLY WAY TO CROSS
1918-1930

Armistice Day 1918 found Cunard bloodied but unbowed, the fleet's first peacetime task being to return thousands of jubilant GIs back home. Miraculously, of its five top Atlantic liners, all but the Lusitania had survived.

By 1925 Cunard had taken delivery of eight new passenger ships, naming most of them after vessels lost in action. Four years earlier it had also acquired the pride of the German fleet, the Imperator, launched by the Kaiser for the Hamburg-America Line in 1912. Renamed the Berengaria, she became the Cunard flagship of the Twenties. Cunard also continued to renew and expand its cargo fleet, opening new routes to take refrigerated meat from Australia to Britain and North America.

Times were changing. As it temporarily loosened its bonds with Europe, America set increasingly tight quotas on immigration although its northern neighbour still encouraged emigrants to 'build their nest in Western Canada'. At the top end of the market, luxury was the name of the game as the Atlantic shipping lines wooed millionaires, aristocrats and celebrities with interiors like palaces and amenities to match. They also won business from the growing numbers of American tourists who wanted to 'do Europe', retrace their emigrant roots or revisit the places that they knew from the War. Cunard set its sights even further afield when in 1922 the Laconia set out on the first ever world cruise.

In designing its new fleet, Cunard took on board the need to cater for these different tastes and aspirations. In its brochure for the Scythia, the shipping line explained: 'There are palatial vessels with all the extreme luxury of the most exclusive of metropolitan hotels. Then there are ships, somewhat of less sumptuous and not of such mighty proportions, which might be compared to the delightful smaller private hotels which every city offers the initiated.' Its five 20,000 ton liners brought the luxury of first class travel to passengers who preferred crossing on smaller ships than the Aquitania and the Mauretania. Space on its six new vessels chiefly for the Canadian trade was allocated primarily to third class and cargo.

At times Cunard struggled to match the elegance of the French Line's Ile de France or the Italian Line's Conte de Savoia. The Mauretania and the Aquitania were beginning to look outmoded. Cunard disguised the faded grandeur of these ocean dowagers by playing the card of British snob appeal with dinner at the Captain's table and strict dress codes de rigeur. While crossing may have been half the fun, certain things were 'simply not done'.

After the Wall Street Crash the bottom fell out of the luxury market. British earnings from the increasingly empty Atlantic more than halved between 1928 and 1931. With economic clouds fast gathering on the horizon, in 1929 Cunard took an immense gamble by deciding to build at least one liner that would outclass any ship on the Atlantic in speed and power. In December, 1930 the contract was signed with John Brown's shipyard on the Clyde for Job No 534.

ALBANIA II
1921-1941

The Albania was the first passenger ship completed for Cunard after the First World War, her keel having been laid down in 1914. She marked the return to the fashion of one huge funnel rather than the four-funnellers of the Edwardian era.

She proved a bit of a lame duck. By the time of her maiden voyage nearly a decade had passed and fashions in interior design had changed. Carrying only cabin class passengers and cargo, she was too small to operate effectively as a passenger liner and too large and luxurious to serve as a freighter. She wintered on the Liverpool-New York route and summered up the St Lawrence to Montreal. When less than five years old she was laid up: another five years passed before she found a buyer, an Italian shipping line. She was torpedoed off Sicily when serving as a hospital ship.

BERENGARIA
1919-1946

In the 1920s the Berengaria was Cunard's flagship and the world's largest liner. She made her first crossing for Cunard in December, 1919 as the Imperator, her name being changed to honour Berengaria, the wife of King Richard the Lionheart, two years later. Passengers and crew christened her 'the Berry'. On inheriting her as compensation for the loss of the Lusitania, Cunard made few changes other than removing no.13 from cabin doors and replacing marble bath tubs with lighter metal ones in an attempt to cure her list.

The décor of this top-heavy lady reflected German ideas of luxury. Passengers who preferred the statelier elegance of liners like the Mauretania christened it 'Berengaria Baroque'. Her captains summed her up as 'a ship of gloomy panelled majesty, hard to handle, clumsy and Teutonic, a creation of industry without pretensions to beauty' and as 'a bejewelled ferryboat for the rich and titled'.

The rich, titled and stars of the silent screen loved her: Mary Pickford, Douglas Fairbanks, Henry Ford, Junius Pierpont Morgan, the Queen of Romania, the Astors, the Vanderbilts and the DuPonts were among the passengers who graced her first class dining room which could seat 900. On one voyage in 1924 her passenger list included a 'Lord Renfrew': passengers who moved in High Society immediately recognised him as Edward Prince of Wales.

Right The first class smoking room was modelled on that of a German baronial hall.

CUNARD LINE - R·M·S· BERENGARIA (*Ex IMPERATOR*)

1st Class Dining Saloon.

1st Class Smoking Room

Palm Court

Lounge

In the early 1930s the Berengaria earned the less elegant nicknames of 'Bargain Area' and 'Dead and Bury'er' when, desperate for any business, she went on weekend booze cruises to earn money from alcohol starved Americans during Prohibition. She also regularly cruised in the Caribbean.

Her last days were plagued by fires due to faulty wiring, After a major incident in New York Harbor in 1938, which took the fire brigade and crew three hours to bring under control, she crossed the Atlantic empty for the last time.

LANCASTRIA
1922-1940

Although she started life as the Tyrrhenia, passengers never liked the name. After a refit to convert her for cruising in 1924, Cunard renamed her Lancastria. She continued on the Liverpool-New York run and the Cabin Channel Service calling at New York, Plymouth, le Havre and London until 1932, when she took to the calmer waters of the Mediterranean and northern Europe as a cruise ship.

Life below deck was hard. Jack Longrigg remembered the daily routine in the 1930s. 'We had to get up at 6.30am and do a 'scrub out' which consisted of scrubbing part of a deck or polishing brasses in the toilets. We had to be standing at table for breakfast at 8am until 9.30am. At 11 o'clock we had to go round the decks with hot drinks for the passengers.

Right In port, 1936.

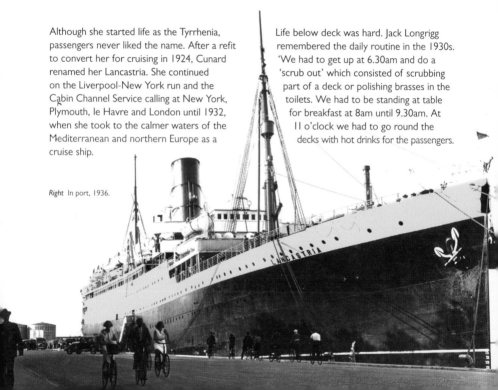

Then we had to attend our tables for lunch from 12.30 to 1.30. Then we had to go around the decks again for afternoon teas at 4pm. Then, dinner from 6.30 to 7.30 . . . '.

On 17th June, 1940 the Lancastria was the subject of the worst disaster in Britain's maritime history. Packed with retreating troops and refugees from war-torn Europe, she was moored off the French port of St Nazaire when a German bomber offloaded its cargo. Four bombs ripped through the ship. The final death toll will never be known, the purser having stopped counting embarking passengers on reaching 6,000. Estimates of losses range from 5,000 to 9,000.

Left The 1930s was the era of the poster. This marine artist chose to illustrate some of the Lancastria's more exotic destinations.

SCYTHIA II
1921-1958

SAMARIA II
1922-1955

The Scythia, Samaria, Laconia and Franconia were the first of a new breed of Cunarders which took to cruising as well as crossing. In 1922 Laconia II was the first passenger liner ever to go on a world cruise and the largest of her era to travel through the Panama Canal.

The Samaria II's first world cruise in 1923 was so successful that it was repeated the following year when the Scythia II made her maiden cruise from New York to the Mediterranean. By the late 1920s their second class accommodation had been renamed 'tourist class' to reflect their new pleasure seeking role.

One passenger on the Scythia II was moved to write to the Daily Telegraph in 1927, 'From all hands we have received the utmost

courtesy and made to feel quite at home from the moment we embarked at New York. The cuisine has exceeded our anticipations - quality, quantity and civility being an outstanding feature. We would also like to emphasise our appreciation of the Scythia's riding qualities and steadiness. We have one regret that the voyage has been too short.'

Above Samaria II.
Right 'Getting to know you'. First class passengers could be assured of only meeting the 'Right People' in the lounge of the Scythia II.

Adriatic, Palestine
Egypt, Italy & Riviera
March *17*
30 days from 52 GNS

LACONIA II
1921-1942

FRANCONIA II
1923-1956

Left Poster for winter cruising on the Laconia, 1937.
Above Soldiers arriving on the Franconia's last voyage as a trooper.

The Laconia and Franconia were named after Cunarders lost during the 1914-18 war. Their fates in the Second World War were very different.

On 12th September, 1942, while carrying Italian prisoners of war in the South Atlantic, the Laconia was torpedoed and sank. The U-boat mounted a rescue operation until hit by a bomb from a US aircraft. The U-boat's Commander responded by cutting loose the string of packed lifeboats which he was towing.

The Franconia's destinations as a troopship sounded even more exotic than her cruising itinerary - Malta, France, India, the Middle East, Cape Town, Madagascar, North Africa, Italy and New York - but the 319,784 miles that she covered were vital to winning the War. Her moment of glory came in 1945 when she acted as Churchill's base during the Yalta Conference with Roosevelt and Stalin to arrange the future of the post-war world.

ANDANIA II
1922-1940

ANTONIA
1922-1948

AUSONIA II
1922-1965

The Antonia was the first of six Cunarders whose names began with A: they were the A-class liners. These smart little vessels were known for their reliability on routes to New York, Halifax, Quebec and Montreal. Oil-fired turbine engines allowed cargo to replace coal in their holds.

Each could carry over 500 cabin class passengers on the upper decks and 1,200 third class passengers in more basic accommodation below. If Cunard compared the Aquitania to the Ritz and the Scythia II to an exclusive private hotel, vessels like the Antonia were very much Atlantic boarding houses. Even in third class, however, life on deck became more fun with a place to stroll, deck chairs with blankets and organised games laid on.

Right The Antonia displayed the might of steam over sail.
Opposite Cunard joined with the Canadian Government in luring emigrants to fill the prairies.

CUNARD
TO CANADA

AURANIA III
1924-1961

ALAUNIA II
1925-1957

ASCANIA II
1925-1956

The first A-class liners proved so successful that Cunard commissioned a second set of triplets.

Of the three, Ascania II had the most adventurous life. In 1934, during an Atlantic storm, she answered a distress call from a stricken British cargo steamer which was taking in water. Sadly the 12 hour search was called off with no trace of wreckage or survivors. A month later she collided with the Canadian-Pacific's Beaverbrae at Quebec and on her next voyage rescued nine crew from the Unsworth which was sinking in mid-Atlantic. In July, 1938, when travelling down the St Lawrence River laden with bullion, she struck the submerged Alcide Rocks, resulting in the flooding of four holds and damage to a propeller. Yet, two months later, she was back in service.

Out of the six As, only the Ascania rejoined the Cunard fleet after the Second World War. The Andania was sunk by a U-boat off Iceland in 1940 while the rest were bought by the Admiralty for conversion into fleet repair ships.

Left Aurania III
Opposite The first class lounge on the Aurania III looking little different from that of a comfortable city hotel.

CARINTHIA II

1925-1940

The Carinthia was one of the first Cunarders designed for cruising in winter. She wore a coat of white paint to keep cool when sailing in tropical waters. While Cunard likened their liners in cruising livery to yachts, the less complimentary among the crews compared them to wedding cakes.

Like the Franconia she aimed for the luxury market, boasting that her first class cabins had instant hot water and beds six inches wider than any other ship afloat. The pair became legends in the Jazz Age, providing inspiration for Cole Porter and Noel Coward lyrics. Both song writers could regularly be found sipping the latest cocktails or lounging on the sun deck - 'Anything Goes'.

'Around the World' ... 'You'll Want the Best' lured travellers to exotic places from Japan to the Norwegian fjords. Postcards home no longer featured the vessel battling the Atlantic waves but moored off a Brazilian port or being greeted by a flotilla of native craft.

Left The Carinthia wore white for cruising.

OLYMPIC QUEENS
1931-1940

11th December, 1931 was one of the darkest days in Cunard's history. Less than a year after the keel of the future Queen Mary was laid at John Brown's shipyard in Clydebank, the Directors called a halt to building. Over 9,000 men were laid off throughout Britain as a result of the decision and the rusting skeleton of Job No. 534 became a national symbol of the Depression.

On 1st January, 1934 the unthinkable happened when Cunard merged with its rival the White Star Line. After protracted Treasury negotiations, the Government agreed to make a repayable loan of £4.5m to Cunard for 534 with the promise of £5m for her projected sister ship, the future Queen Elizabeth, provided the two shipping lines joined forces. By creating one strong Atlantic shipping line – Cunard-White Star – it hoped to avoid having to bail out both rivals independently.

In 1926 the Royal Mail Line had bought White Star back into British ownership but an elderly fleet and a dramatic fall in Atlantic traffic had brought the line to its knees. Although technically a merger, in practice Cunard was the winner. The White Star order for Job No. 844, the Oceanic, already under construction, was cancelled. By 1936 there were only two White Star liners still at sea – the Georgic and the Laurentic – which sailed for Cunard until the mid 1950s.

After Easter, 1934 work on 534 restarted and five months later, the Queen Mary was launched by Queen Mary, the wife of George V, amid intense speculation about her name. The launch was a truly national event, the London Times summing up both the mood and the challenge: 'It is customary for Great Britain to construct from time to time such ships as are necessary to maintain her ancient predominance on the seas.'

The new challenger was the French Line's Normandie which entered service in 1935. 'The grand French lady' was large, fast and beautiful, her many admirers claiming that the Blue Riband winner was the most elegant ship ever built. The Queen Mary set out on her maiden voyage on 27th May, 1936 to a tumultuous farewell and ecstatic reviews. She soon not only captured the Blue Riband for Britain with a westward crossing of four days, seven hours and twelve minutes but won the hearts of passengers, crew and the public, becoming a true British institution.

The designers of the second Cunard super-liner, the future Queen Elizabeth, set out to outclass the Normandie. Her two funnels and sleek lines gave her a more contemporary look while her streamlined hull delivered more speed for less power. Eight long years of world upheaval were to pass, however, before the public had their first sight of the marvels of her interior. Launched during the Munich crisis of 1938, she secretly slipped from the Clyde half-finished in 1940 to free her shipyard to build warships. For two weeks, the world's three greatest liners – the Queens and the Normandie – lay in adjoining berths in New York Harbor before the two Queens departed on war duties round the world, later playing a crucial role in winning the Battle of the Atlantic.

METROPOLITAN TOWER — NEW YORK. 700 FEET HIGH

NEW WOOLWORTH BUILDING NEW YORK. 750 FEET HIGH

R.M.S. "OLYMPIC" 882·6 FEET LONG

COLOGNE CATHEDRAL COLOGNE. 516 FEET HIGH

GRAND PYRAMID GIZEH. AFRICA. 451 FEET HIGH

WHITE STAR LINE R.M.S "OLYMPIC"
COMPARED WITH VARIOUS FAMOUS BUILDINGS.

OLYMPIC

1934-1937

The Olympic was the first of a trio of White Star liners, completed on the same day as her tragic sister was launched. After the sinking of the Titanic during her maiden voyage in 1912, the Olympic was hastily refitted with a double hull and room on a lifeboat for all passengers, at enormous cost.

The largest and most luxurious liner of her day, the Olympic proved very popular with passengers and crew: her longest serving captain, Sir Bertram Hayes, described her as 'the finest ship in my estimation that has ever been built or ever will be'. During the First World War, troops knew her affectionately as 'Old Reliable'.

Her life was not without incident. In 1918 she became the only merchant vessel to sink an enemy warship during the First World War, when she fired on U-boat U-103. In 1924 a collision with another liner in New York Harbor necessitated the replacement of her stern frame, an operation never before carried out on so large a vessel. Five years later she shook continuously for two minutes as she sailed over the Grand Banks earthquake and in 1934 she collided with the Nantucket lightship, with the loss of seven of its 11 crew. The next year, in the depths of the Depression she was reduced to offering day trips from Southampton. The 'For Sale' sign was hoisted but no-one wanted her and so she sailed under her own steam to the breaker's yard.

Left Built for the White Star line in 1911, the Olympic was a match for her contemporary, New York's Woolworth Building, which held the record as the world's tallest building until overshadowed by the Chrysler Building in 1929.

MAJESTIC II
1934-1939

The Majestic was originally Hamburg Amerika Line's Bismarck, launched by the Iron Chancellor's granddaughter in 1914. She was designed to outrival the Mauretania or the Titanic in the battle for supremacy of the Atlantic. Given to White Star in compensation for the loss of the Britannic in 1916, she remained the world's largest liner until the maiden voyage of the Normandie in 1935.

Nicknamed 'the Magic Stick', she served on the Southampton-New York run interspersed with short cruises during the Depression. Carrying a mere 500 passengers was a very different experience to that of a decade before when she set a new White Star record in 1923 with 2,625 passengers on board. Not everyone, however, was wanted on the voyage. An escaped monkey once delayed her departure from New York and an adventurous nine year old girl managed to stowaway twice.

In 1934 she was the first liner to enter the new Southampton graving dock, built in anticipation of handling monsters like the Queen Mary. Two years later she made her last crossing, ending her days as a cadet training ship. The era of floating palaces and the three-ship Atlantic express service was over.

Above The Majestic enters New York in her White Star days.
Right Even White Star tourist class passengers had the chance to 'meet in the street' on the promenade deck of the world's largest liner.

GEORGIC

1934-1956

Left Operations to right the stricken ship.
Above The Georgic at sea.

The Georgic was the last White Star liner. One of a new generation of 'motorships', diesel power and improved means of internal ventilation meant that funnels became as much a design feature as a necessity. The Georgic's sleek rounded lines and squat funnels captured the spirit of the Art Deco era, the second funnel serving as the engineers' lounge.

The Georgic was a survivor. In July 1941, when at anchor in Port Tewfik on the Suez Canal, two bombs set her stern alight. Having successfully beached the blazing ship and evacuated the passengers, including 800 Italian prisoners of war, her captain left her to meet her fate. So desperate were the Allies for ships, however, that she was raised, repaired and by 1945 was back on active service. The Georgic never quite recovered from her wartime experience. Her battle scars included the loss of a funnel and structural defects that meant that she could no longer sail the Atlantic in winter.

CHURCHMAN'S CIGARETTES

THE "QUEEN MARY": PLATING IN PROGRESS AT BOWS

QUEEN MARY
1936-1967

'Built for the arts of peace and to link the Old World with the New, the Queens challenged the fury of Hitlerism in the Battle of the Atlantic. Without their aid the day of final victory must unquestionably have been postponed.'

Sir Winston Churchill, 1946.

Left The Queen Mary steaming into New York at the end of her maiden voyage accompanied by a flotilla of pleasure craft, tugs and fire boats.
Above Plating a Queen - one of a series of fifty Churchman's cigarette cards designed to satisfy the public's insatiable appetite for information about the world's largest liner.

Elegant and modern, the Queen Mary was the epitome of Art Deco at sea. Although the style celebrated 'the machine age', achieving it demanded impeccable craftsmanship to combine the elegant materials and execute the painstaking detail. Artists, metal workers and carvers created the interiors of the 'Ship of Beautiful Woods' whose thirty species included cedar and satinwood.

Only four years after her maiden voyage all the finery was stripped out and replaced by dormitories of standee bunks where soldiers slept in shifts, as the world's fastest liner was refitted as a troop ship. In July, 1943 she carried the greatest number of people on board a ship - 16,683 - a record unbroken to this day.

Left Passengers sipped pre-dinner cocktails as they watched the ocean from the Observation lounge with its Art Deco bar.
Right First class passengers made an entrance through bronze doors to dine under a huge map where a crystal model of the ship moved to indicate her route.

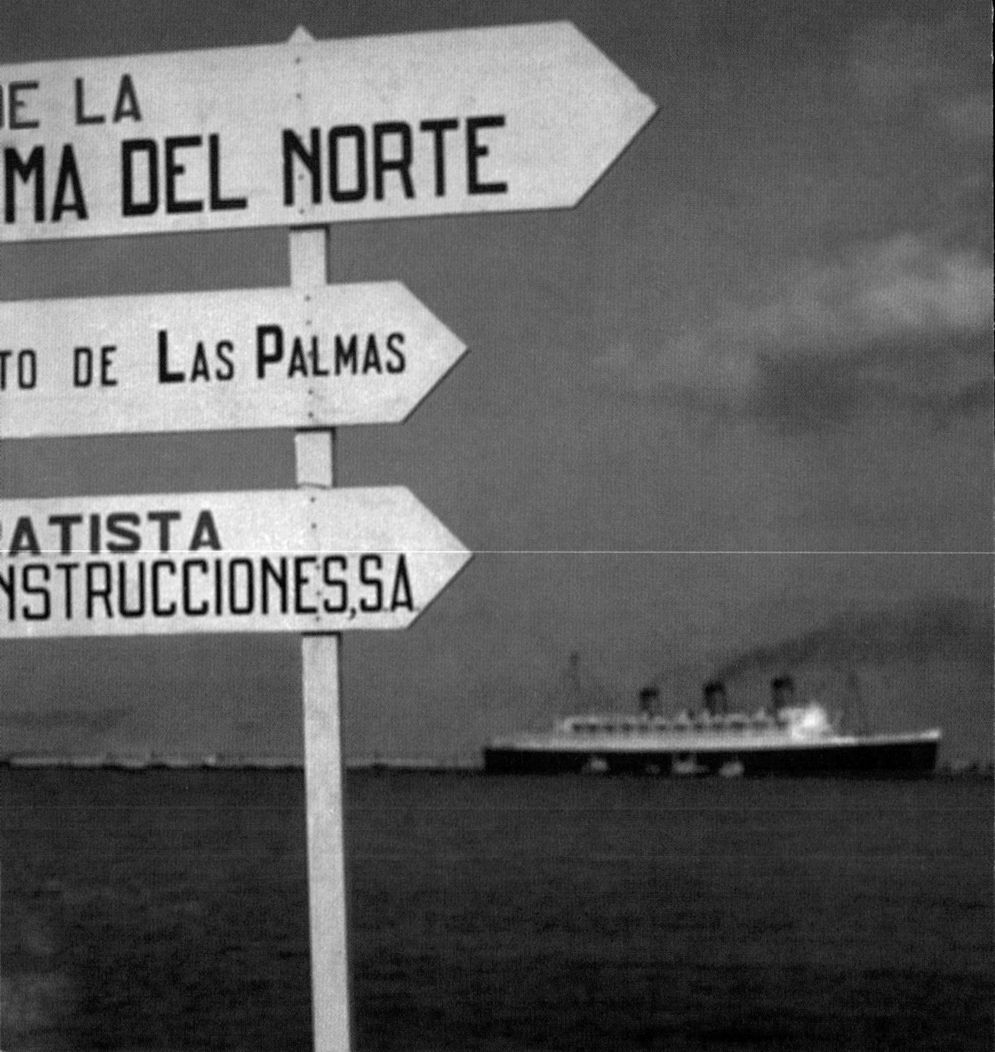
E LA
MA DEL NORTE
TO DE LAS PALMAS
ATISTA
NSTRUCCIONES,SA

For much of her career, the Queen Mary was *the* ship on which to cross or cruise, her passenger lists reading like a 'Who's Who' of the titled, the moneyed and the glamorous. Cecil Beaton took photographs while Bing Crosby relaxed with the developers in the dark room. Clark Gable broke susceptible hearts and Cary Grant met one of his five wives on board. Bob Hope practised his golf swing and a young Elizabeth Taylor walked her dogs on deck.

By the mid 1960s fewer and fewer passengers remained faithful to the ageing Queen. On 27th September, 1967 she sailed into Southampton for the last time with 1,400 passengers on board. The captain's table was graced with Cherbourg sole and chrysanthemums and the band played Auld Lang Syne. On board, travelling incognito, was John Brown who as a young naval architect had helped to design the Queens. Queen Mary ended her sailing days in 1967 and is now a floating hotel and museum in Long Beach, California.

Top In their years of exile after Edward VIII's abdication the Windsors added a touch of poignant glamour to the Queen Mary. *Opposite* Cruising in the Canaries.

QUEEN ELIZABETH
1940-1968

The maiden voyage of the Queen Elizabeth was very different from that of her sister. The press embargo was lifted only when she had arrived safely in New York. The headlines were sombre - 'A lady in half mourning'. 'Not a flag flying'.

When the Second World War broke out, the Queen Elizabeth lay half fitted out in John Brown's shipyard, Clydebank. There were concerns that the world's largest liner would be an obvious target from the air. Under the guise of making for Southampton for sea trials, the untested Queen slipped into the North Atlantic, her engines working perfectly.

After a brief sojourn in New York she headed for Singapore to be converted into a troopship. From August 1942, she shuttled across the Atlantic carrying 10,000 troops on each crossing.

Left The majestic bow rising above John Brown's shipyard, Clydebank.
Right The world's three greatest liners (from left Normandie, Queen Mary and Queen Elizabeth) in New York, 1940.

From 1946 the Queen Elizabeth revealed her true colours as she set out on her maiden voyage to New York. The power of the two super-liners was such that Cunard could offer a two-ship, weekly relay across the Atlantic, the Queens regularly saluting each other in mid ocean.

In the early 1950s the Queen Elizabeth was fully booked months in advance. Over 1,200 crew worked long hours to ensure that the liner kept to timetable and that the 2,280 passengers enjoyed the comforts of 'a grand English country house'. Cunard occasionally allowed passengers a glimpse of life below deck. 'High St QE is the address of a butcher,

a fishmonger, a poulterer, a baker who can make his own yeast, a shop which has nearly 200,000 pieces of linen on hand, a plumber, a fire station, a police office, a wages office, a hospital, a newspaper, a couple of pubs (strictly unofficial) and a book maker.'

By the end of the decade, however, more passengers were crossing by air than by sea. From 1963 the Queen took to cruising in a bid to earn money. Despite a complete makeover and the installation of an open-air swimming pool, however, her fate was sealed.

Above Bellboys lined up for inspection.
Opposite Elizabeth meeting Liberty at the entrance to New York Harbor.

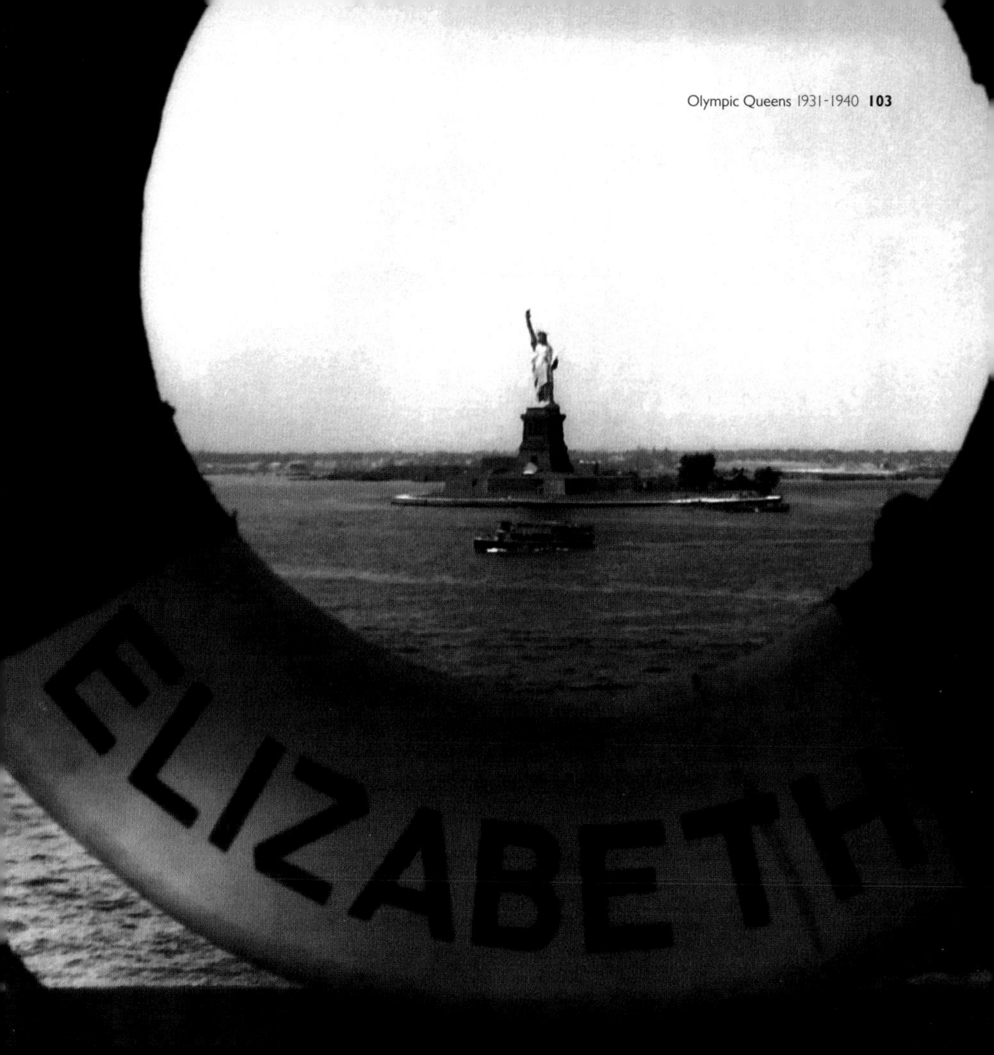
ELIZABETH

During the 1960s it was possible to be the only person in the lounge for afternoon tea, as the leisurely Queen Elizabeth lost out to the glamour and speed of air travel. In 1968, with the QE2 waiting in the wings, Cunard withdrew her from service. After a brief reign as a floating hotel in Port Everglades, Florida, she was auctioned to the highest bidder, Taiwanese businessman C.Y. Tung, and sailed to Hong Kong to be converted into a floating University.

On 9th January, 1972, when several fires broke out on board, arson was suspected although the culprit was never caught. By next morning she lay on her side in Hong Kong harbour. Three years later, on Guy Fawkes Day (November 5th), the once glorious Queen had enough of the arguments about her future: she rolled over and sank below the waves.

BUILT FOR THE SUN
1946-1996

With the last GIs returned to America and 40,000 war brides and their babies dispatched to their new homes, it was back to business on the Atlantic. Cunard paid a heavy price for war service, being expected to contribute a third of the £7.5m bill to refurbish the Queens, the Mauretania and the Britannic as well as the cost of replacing vessels lost in action. The troops had taken a heavy toll on teak decks and staterooms and had left their mark in the shape of millions of graffiti.

Rapidly escalating building costs and the untimely death of Cunard's inspired Chairman who had steered the Queens through the 1930s compounded the problem. Percy Bates died on the very morning that he was due to join the Queen Elizabeth on her maiden voyage. Her captain, Commodore James Bisset, paid tribute: the Queens 'were the children of his brain. He lived for them, he worked for them, he wore himself out with anxieties for them, and he has died for them'.

Dropping White Star from its name, the shipping line forecast that its long term future lay in cruising as much as crossing. Its new ships like the Caronia II were equipped with outdoor pools and sun decks and a growing programme of leisure activities from keep fit to the latest films.

The prosperous 1950s were the golden years of the liners with a third of passengers choosing to cross on the largest, fastest and most famous ships on the Atlantic. 1958 was a record breaking year, with 1.2m Atlantic travellers overall and 70% of Cunard passengers voyaging for pleasure. It was also the year when Pan American Airways launched the first trans-Atlantic flights, reducing the journey time between London and New York to seven hours. By the end of 1959 the liner trade had lost a quarter of its passengers.

Believing that its rival in the skies would simply increase the overall travel market, Cunard's solution was another Queen or even two. The tide, however, was turning in favour of the jet set. Increasingly, elderly passengers complained about the service and harked back to 'the good old days' while the press talked of 'Cunard-on-Sea', likening a crossing to a wet Sunday in a deserted seaside resort. After a brief flirtation with running an airline, and years of cancelled contracts and arguments with the Government over ship finance, Cunard finally announced the Q4 project in 1963. Six years later the QE2 set out on her maiden voyage, the only Queen left and widely tipped to be the last Atlantic liner.

At first the QE2 lost money and for a time it looked as if Cunard might withdraw from the passenger business altogether. By the late 1970s, with four new purpose designed ships and the QE2 refitted for a more leisurely lifestyle, Cunard found new vigour as a cruise shipping line. In 1985 air and sea were finally reconciled when Cunard partnered Concorde, the world's first supersonic aircraft, in offering travellers the trip of a lifetime.

The Cunarders still abandoned their cruise schedules for wartime duties. In 1982, when Britain and Argentina went to war over disputed ownership of the Falkland Islands, the QE2, the Saxonia and two Cunard container ships headed for the South Atlantic. In 1991 Cunard Princess was chartered to the US Government to provide a respite base for frontline troops in the Gulf War. Three years later, the QE2 and the Vistafjord performed happier military duties in the celebrations to mark the 50th anniversary of D-Day.

MEDIA
1947-1989

The Media was the first new passenger ship on the Atlantic after the end of the War. Originally designed as a freighter for the Brocklebank Line, Cunard bought her and her sister the Parthia and converted them into combined cargo-passenger vessels, a unique formula in the shipping line's history.

She was popular for her leisurely 8-10 day crossings, longer stays in New York and the greater intimacy of having only 250 passengers, all first-class, on board. The downside was that she rolled and pitched in rough seas. In 1952 she became the first ship on the North Atlantic to be fitted with fin stabilisers. So much smoother was the passage that Cunard decided to install the new stabilisers on all its liners.

After Cunard sold her in 1961, the Media continued her career, serving as an emigrant ship on the Australian run and later as a cruise ship in the Caribbean.

Opposite Aerial view of the Media (left) alongside the Queen Mary and the Britannic against the gridplan of New York.

MAURETANIA II
1939-1965

The Mauretania II was essentially a ship of the 1950s. She only made three crossings before taking up duties as a troopship, transporting ANZACS to Suez, India and Singapore and GIs to Europe.

With her two funnels and late Art Deco style, the Mauretania was a first cousin to the Queen Elizabeth while in luxury and service she looked back to the great days of her namesake. Certain Cunard traditions died hard: about 10.30 each morning, the captain met with senior staff to decide which passengers merited the privilege of sitting at which officer's table that day. Boy's birthdays were marked with a resounding chorus of 'For he's a jolly good fellow' and roast beef and Yorkshire pudding was a favourite on the menu.

Although her pre-war run had been London-New York, making her the largest ship ever to navigate the Thames, from 1947 she switched to Southampton-New York and dollar earning cruises in the West Indies. In 1962, painted a relaxed pale green and with her passenger accommodation remodelled, she largely took to cruising. Even that, however, did not pay and three years later she was scrapped.

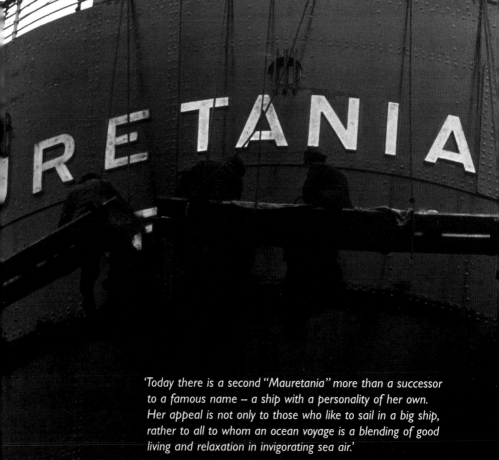

'Today there is a second "Mauretania" more than a successor to a famous name -- a ship with a personality of her own. Her appeal is not only to those who like to sail in a big ship, rather to all to whom an ocean voyage is a blending of good living and relaxation in invigorating sea air.'

Cunard publicity

CARONIA II
1949-1974

The Caronia II was the world's first purpose built cruise ship. She was designed to look like a yacht with her clipper bow, single funnel and the highest tripod mast of her time. Sun worshippers could lounge on her terraced decks and open air lido or cool off in the first outdoor pool on a Cunarder. Six of her lifeboats doubled as ferries to shuttle passengers ashore.

She set off on her first world itinerary in 1951 with 30 far-flung ports of call. She soon gained a reputation as one of the most luxurious ships afloat. In numbers the crew almost matched her 900 passengers and her hand-picked-stewards always wore crisp white jackets. Some millionaires cruised so frequently that they brought their own furniture and pictures to make their stateroom feel like home. The Caronia played on Americans' love of a royal. Pictures of Princess Elizabeth and the Duke of Edinburgh, who had travelled on the Caronia during her sea trials, dominated the main lounge and the restaurants were named Balmoral and Sandringham after the royal palaces. Her royal associations were strengthened in 1953 when she was chartered to take Americans to the Coronation.

Opposite Princess Elizabeth launching the Caronia in 1947 in recognition of the wartime service of the Queens. It was her last public engagement before her marriage.
Above The 'Green Goddess' sporting her tropical livery.

SAXONIA II
1954-1969

IVERNIA II
1955-

Launched in 1954 by the wife of Winston Churchill, the Saxonia was the first of a completely new class of Cunarder. Close in her wake came her sisters the Ivernia, the Carinthia and the Sylvania, all designed for the Canadian emigrant trade.

Although they attracted a loyal following, some first class passengers dismissed them as 'flashy' and downmarket: Cunard had decided to give them a modern look with lighter coloured woods and more informal furnishings. In the later two sisters, Cunard reverted to a more traditional style, even re-using the Aquitania's chairs, dating from 1914, in the first class dining room.

In the early 1960s Cunard decided to convert the Saxonia and the Ivernia for cruising, adding lidos, sun terraces and kidney-shaped open air pools. It tested out ideas for the coming super-liner, the future QE2. They were given new identities, the Saxonia being renamed the Carmania and the Ivernia the Franconia III. At first they wore the same green livery as the legendary Caronia although they later reverted to white.

At the height of the swinging sixties, however, the new generation of cruise passengers preferred the more 'with it' ships of foreign competitors. In the early 1970s the 'For Sale' sign went up and the ships eventually transferred to a Russian shipping line.

Right The print room on the Ivernia where the daily menus were produced.
Above A poignant photograph of the Saxonia with an old fashioned example of the ultimate victor of the race for the Atlantic flying overhead.

CARINTHIA III
1956-

SYLVANIA II
1957-2004

The Carinthia and the Sylvania, the last liners
built purely for the North Atlantic, completed
the quartet. Cunard could now offer six
sailings a month to Canada. Only five years
later the Carinthia was the only Cunarder
left on the Canadian service after the Sylvania
replaced the ageing Britannic on the Liverpool-
New York route.

Desperate for ideas to attract new custom in
1967, Cunard experimented by equipping the
Sylvania with an onboard hovercraft to ferry
passengers to shore excursions. Only months
later both ships were withdrawn from service
and sold to an Italian shipping line who re-
equipped them with theatres, night clubs and
additional swimming pools for a more leisurely
style of travel.

Above A far travelled postcard of the Sylvania II franked
in Quebec.
Right Carinthia creating waves on her maiden voyage.

QUEEN ELIZABETH 2
1969-

The QE2 was a reluctant Queen. John Brown's shipyard had been secretly working on drawings for a new ship to replace the Queen Mary since 1947. Ten long years, however, of negotiations and cancellations passed between Cunard's announcement of a new liner in 1959 and the maiden voyage of the QE2.

Her design was a dramatic departure, catching the upbeat mood of the Swinging Sixties. HRH Princes Margaret saw her as a symbol of change: 'This new Cunarder will show that design in Britain is exciting and full of vigorous common sense - is always out in front, leading the field.'

Although much admired for her sleek, elegant lines, controversy raged over her funnel. Instead of traditional Cunard red and black, the QE2 sported one rakish, thin funnel, painted white in keeping with her bold design. A second funnel to ventilate the kitchen was cleverly hidden in her mast.

Left Fitting the bridge into place on Job No. 736.
Above The futuristic Queen's Room of the QE2 where couples danced the night away.

The QE2 was built for cruising, spending some of the year on the Atlantic run and the rest in pursuit of the sun. Cunard Line corrected any misconceptions: 'She is not a modern version of the Queens. She is a resort hotel that has the advantage of being able to follow the sun.'

In 1975, the QE2 went on her first world cruise. The round trip involved a journey of 38,000 miles: between Antigua and Boston, the liner celebrated her millionth mile since her maiden voyage.

In 1985 the ocean finally made peace with the air when Concorde joined the QE2 on a world cruise. Preparation for the voyage was immaculate, Captain Woodall being dispatched in September, 1983 'with a thick folder full of

airline tickets, a fistful of dollars and a case of charts'. During his 52 day journey he visited 28 cities, clocked up 38,700 air miles and checked that the Queen could sail through the Panama Canal. It was a tight fit with less than two feet to spare on either side.

The QE2 has now travelled the same distance as nine times to the moon and back.

Above The QE2 was designed to fit into the Panama Canal with only 18 inches to spare on either side.

CUNARD COUNTESS
1976-

CUNARD PRINCESS
1977-

Cruising Cunard style was here to stay.
In the early 1970s the company flirted with
fly-cruise holidays by partnering an airline
in commissioning two new vessels, Cunard
Adventurer and Cunard Ambassador. The
careers of these ships, bought by Cunard after
the airline encountered financial difficulties,
were brief. The Adventurer was sold to
another shipping line and the Ambassador
ended her days transporting sheep.

Their replacements were Cunard Countess
and Cunard Princess. These were ships
for the stars, their design being initiated by
Hollywood's MGM Studios as part of an
abortive plan to broaden its interests. Cunard
modified the concept for Caribbean cruising.

The wife of astronaut Neil Armstrong, the
first person to walk on the Moon, named the
Countess. Princess Grace of Monaco, the
former film star Grace Kelly, christened her
namesake, after Cunard decided to drop the
name Conqueror as not befitting a lady. Her
daughter Princess Caroline christened a later
Cunard cruise ship.

During their careers with Cunard, both ships
also served their country, the Countess as a
troopship during the Falklands conflict of 1982
and the Princess as a respite centre for troops
in the Gulf War of 1991.

Opposite Princess Grace blessing her namesake, 1977.

CARONIA III

1983-

Left The QE2 and Caronia III basking in the glow of a tropical sunset.

With the purchase of the Norwegian American Line in 1983, Cunard Line inherited two vessels, the Sagafjord and the Vistafjord. Under the Cunard flag they consistently won top star ratings from cruise reviewers. By the mid 1990s Cunard was operating six of the world's top eleven cruise ships.

The two elegant smaller vessels with their classic lines and high ratio of crew to passengers provided the atmosphere of a country club at sea. Passengers chose to make their home on them as they roamed the world's oceans calling in at ports from Spitzbergen within the Arctic Circle to South Seas islands.

In honour of the luxurious 'Green Goddess', the Vistafjord was rechristened the Caronia III in 1999, keeping up the tradition of being the only member of the fleet to be named after an American. The first Caronia had honoured Caro Brown, whose grandfather was Cunard's New York agent at the turn of the 20th century.

A NEW QUEEN FOR
A NEW MILLENNIUM

1997-2004

When the QE2 set out on her maiden voyage in 1969, most people thought that she would be the last Atlantic liner. With supersonic Concorde, the jet set could soon breakfast in London and lunch in New York. Ocean travel was consigned to the deep.

Thirty five years later Cunard Line was building Queen Mary 2 and the Concorde fleet was making its last flights. Although travellers no longer had to cross by ship, their centuries-old love affair with the sea was far from over. Ships still symbolised the ultimate in elegance and romance.

In November, 2000 Cunard Line signed the contract for Job No. G32 with the ALSTOM-Chantiers de l'Atlantique shipyard which has been building Atlantic liners since the 1860s in the French Atlantic port of St Nazaire. The keel was laid six months later, 162 years to the day since the Britannia set out on her maiden voyage. At the launch ceremony 600-ton Block No. 502, one of 94 that make up QM2's hull, was lowered into place. Two coins were welded to the base of the mast in a tradition that dates back to Roman times.

On 12th January 2004 Queen Mary 2 set sail on her 14 day maiden voyage from Southampton to Fort Lauderdale, Florida after the traditional send-off of fireworks and cheering crowds. The Nautical Institute and Lloyd's List awarded her the honour of 'Ship of the Year' for setting a new benchmark in ocean transport.

Three months later, one era ended and another began as QM2 departed from New York on her maiden eastbound crossing in tandem with the QE2 on her very last crossing of the Atlantic. It was the first time that two Cunard Queens had berthed together in New York since March 1940 and that two Cunarders had crossed the Atlantic within sight of each other since 1967.

On arrival in Southampton, Queen Mary 2 put on the mantle of flagship, designed to rule the oceans for the next forty years, while QE2 began her graceful retirement as Queen Mother.

QM2
2004-

From bow to bridge, putting QM2 together involved 300,000 parts and close on a 1,000 miles of welding. Some parts were measured in inches while others were 35 yards long and weighed 400 tons. Over 20,000 people were directly involved in constructing the vessel in less than two years: it took the equivalent of a million hours to design her and eight million hours to build her.

Her revolutionary design bridges the very different worlds of an Atlantic crossing and a floating resort. Unlike cruise ships, which are designed for shallow waters, the long slender lines of this 150,000 ton Queen, her thick steel hull and the sheer power of her four pods, which both propel and steer her, allow her to slice gracefully and confidently through the Atlantic waves.

Left On 8th January, 2004 Her Majesty Queen Elizabeth II named QM2 in Southampton.
Opposite Welding 'Queen Mary 2' on QM2.

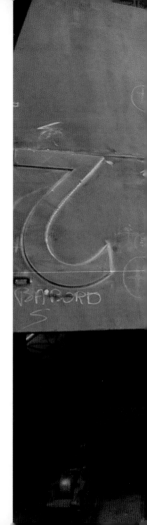

Left Longer than the Eiffel Tower is tall, a foot higher than London's Tower Bridge, the sheer majesty of QM2 defies the imagination. The book 'Queen Mary 2 Book of Comparisons' follows a century-old Cunard tradition of comparing its liners to the man-made and natural wonders of the world.

Queen Mary 2 is the longest, tallest, widest, largest and most expensive passenger vessel ever built.

True to the Cunard tradition, QM2 is a record breaker while maintaining Samuel Cunard's original commitment to safety first. She boasts the largest ballroom, library and wine cellar on the ocean and the first Planetarium, al fresco cinema and permanent exhibition at sea. She also provides the setting for the largest ocean art gallery with works from 128 countries.

Over her 40 year lifetime, she will sail the equivalent of twelve times to the moon and back.

Opposite QM2 makes her New York debut to the traditional salute from fire boats and helicopters.

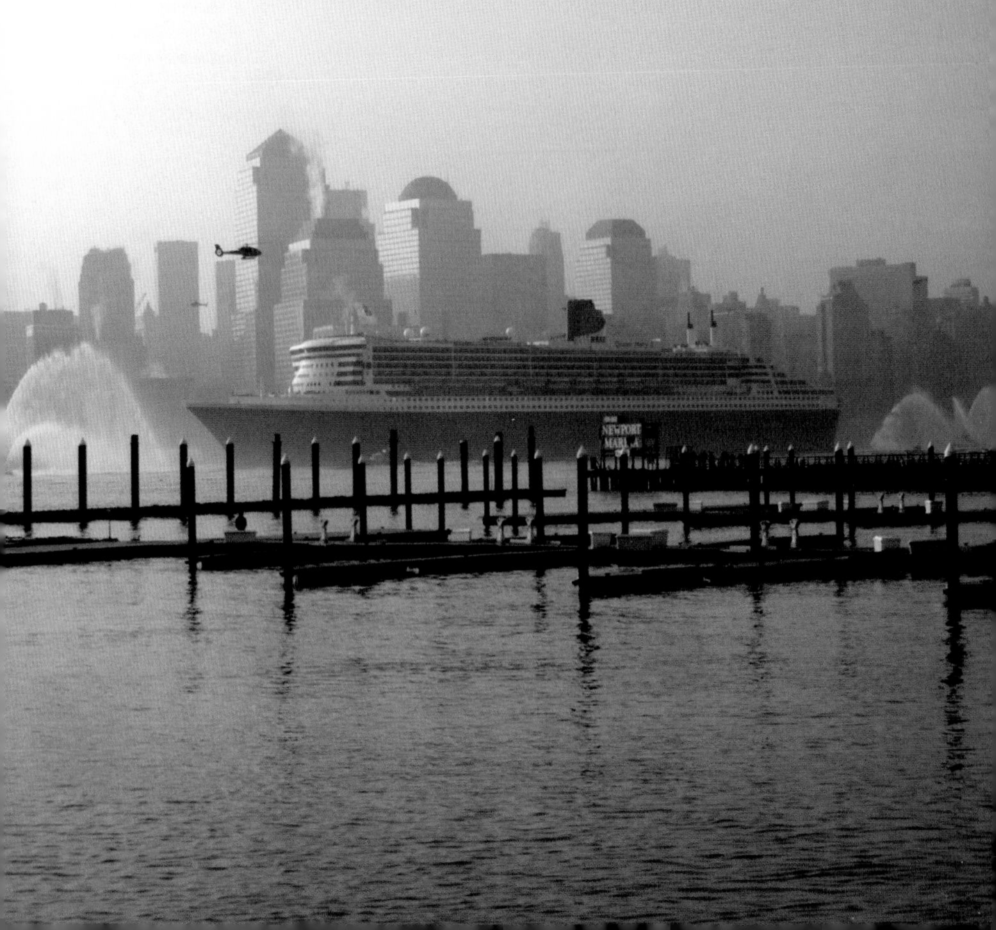
NEWPORT

The popularity of Queen Mary 2 has shown that people still yearn to travel in style on a great ocean liner, to dine, dance and gaze up at the stars.

Samuel Cunard, with his 'plain and comfortable ships', would be astonished at the sumptuous interiors, the exotic dishes and the sheer variety of ways in which passengers choose to pass the time on board the ships that still proudly bear his name. People can even stargaze in the comfort of the world's first Planetarium at sea.

He would, however, have been quietly proud of founding a 165 year tradition borne by a 200 strong fleet from the first tiny paddle steamers to the mighty Queens. That time-honoured tradition will continue as new Cunarders part the waves of the stormy Atlantic or grace the calm waters of a starlit sea.

THE FLEET A-Z

Abyssinia

Gross tonnage 3,376
Dimensions - m 110.7 x 12.9
Builder J & G Thomson, Glasgow
Maiden voyage 1870
Career Had over a thousand emigrant berths. Sold to Guion Line, 1880. Destroyed by fire at sea in 1891 with no casualties.

Acadia

Gross tonnage 1,154
Dimensions - m 63 x 10.4
Builder John Wood, Port Glasgow
Maiden voyage 1840
Career One of the first four Cunarders. Sold to a German shipping line in 1848: chartered by British Government for Crimean War. Scrapped in 1858.

Africa

Gross tonnage 2,226
Dimensions - m 81.1 x 12.2
Builder Robert Steele & Co, Greenock
Maiden voyage 1850
Career Last Cunard wooden paddle steamer to cross the Atlantic. Sold in 1868.

Alaunia

Gross tonnage 13,405
Dimensions - m 158.6 x 19.5
Builder Scott's of Greenock
Maiden voyage 1913
Career One of the first Cunarders to be built for the Canadian emigrant service. Sank after striking a mine in 1916 with two casualties.

Alaunia II

Gross tonnage 14,040
Dimensions - m 157.4 x 19.7
Builder John Brown's, Clydebank
Maiden voyage 1925
Career Built for Canadian service. Sold to the Admiralty as a fleet repair ship, 1944. Scrapped in 1957.

Albania

Gross tonnage 7,640
Dimensions - m 140.7 x 15.9
Builder Swan Hunter, Newcastle
Maiden voyage Bought by Cuanrd, 1911
Career Found not to be up to Cunard's standard and sold to the Bank Line a year later. Scrapped in 1930.

Albania II

Gross tonnage 12,768
Dimensions - m 159.4 x 19.5
Builder Scott's of Greenock
Maiden voyage 1921
Career Construction interrupted by WWI when converted to a freighter. Redesigned as passenger ship but not successful as a liner. Sold in 1930 to Italian Line and sunk by British torpedo in 1941.

Aleppo

Gross tonnage 2,056
Dimensions - m 89.2 x 11.6
Builder J & G Thomson, Glasgow
Maiden voyage 1865
Career Initially on North Atlantic route but from 1872 largely on Mediterranean service. Scrapped in 1909.

Algeria

Gross tonnage 3,428
Dimensions - m 110.1 x12.5
Builder J & G Thomson, Glasgow
Maiden voyage 1870
Career Sailed Liverpool-New York. Sold to Red Star Line, 1882 and scrapped in 1903.

Alps

Gross tonnage 1,440
Dimensions - m 72.1 x 10.1
Builder William Denny and Bros, Dumbarton
Maiden voyage 1852
Career With sister ship the Andes, the first Cunarder to be built of iron and to be driven by screw propeller. Used as hospital ship in Crimean War and thereafter on Mediterranean service. Sold in 1859.

America

Gross tonnage 1,826
Dimensions - m 76.5 x 11.8
Builder Robert Steele & Co., Greenock
Maiden voyage 1848
Career One of Samuel's second generation steamers, held the Liverpool-Boston speed record for several years. Sold in 1866 and converted as sailing vessel Coalgacondor. Scrapped in 1875.

Andania

Gross tonnage 13,405
Dimensions - m 158.9 x 19.5
Builder Scott's of Greenock
Maiden voyage 1913
Career The first of three purpose-built vessels for the Canadian trade. Served as a troop ship and German POW prison hulk in the Thames during WWI. Hit by a torpedo and sunk, 1918.

Andania II

Gross tonnage 13,950
Dimensions - m 158.6 x 19.9
Builder Hawthorn Leslie & Co, Newcastle
Maiden voyage 1922
Career Built for the Canadian emigrant and cargo trade. Laid up during the Depression. Survived a four-torpedo attack in 1940 for long enough for most crew to be picked up by an Icelandic trawler.

Andes

Gross tonnage 1,440
Dimensions - m 72.1 x 10.1
Builder William Denny & Bros, Dumbarton
Maiden voyage 1852
Career One of Cunard's first ships with a screw propeller. Maiden voyage aborted mid-Atlantic due to engine trouble. After serving in Crimean War served in Mediterranean before being sold to Spanish Government in 1859.

Antonia

Gross tonnage 13,867
Dimensions - m 158.5 x 19.9
Builder Vickers Ltd, Barrow
Maiden voyage 1922
Career Served primarily as an emigrant ship on the Canadian run. After trooping and taking evacuated British children to Canada, became an Admiralty fleet repair ship in 1942. Broken up in 1948.

Aquitania

Gross tonnage 45,647
Dimensions - m 264.8 x 29.6
Builder John Brown's, Clydebank
Maiden voyage 1914
Career Claimed to be the world's largest liner. Longest-lived Cunarder of the 20th century, serving in both World Wars. Chartered to Canadian Government as emigrant ship before being broken up in 1949.

Arabia

Gross tonnage 2,402
Dimensions - m 86.6 x 12.5
Builder Robert Steele & Co, Greenock
Maiden voyage 1853
Career Served as trooper in Crimean War carrying horses for the Charge of the Light Brigade. Collided with fellow Cunarder, Europa, in 1858 off Cape Race. Sold and converted to sailing ship in 1864. Sank in 1868.

Ascania

Gross tonnage 9,111
Dimensions - m 142.3 x 17.1
Builder Swan Hunter, Newcastle
Maiden voyage 1911
Career Begun as Gerona for Thomson Line but finished for Cunard. One of three Cunarders to sail from Southampton, up the St Lawrence to Montreal. Wrecked off Newfoundland, 1918 with no casualties.

Ascania II

Gross tonnage 14,013
Dimensions - m 158.5 x 19.9
Builder Armstrong Whitworth, Newcastle
Maiden voyage 1925
Career In winter 1934/5, involved in two rescues and a collision at sea. Active in the Sicily/Italian landings during WW2 and returned evacuees to Gibraltar. Scrapped, 1956 after transporting troops during the Suez Crisis.

Asia

Gross tonnage 2,226
Dimensions - m 81.1 x 12.2
Builder Robert Steele & Co., Greenock
Maiden voyage 1850
Career The largest ship built on the Clyde before 1850. Met increased demand on the New York run. Sold in 1867 and converted to sail. Sank in Bombay after a fire in 1876.

Athenia

Gross tonnage 13,465
Dimensions - m 159.4 x 20.1
Builder Fairfield Shipbuilding, Glasgow
Maiden voyage 1923
Career Commissioned by Anchor Line/Cunard, largely serving Montreal route. In 1935 ownership transferred to Anchor Donaldson. In 1939 it was first British passenger ship to be torpedoed and sunk in WW2.

Atlas

Gross tonnage 2,393
Dimensions - m 100.3 x 11.1
Builder J & G Thomson, Glasgow
Maiden voyage 1873
Career Originally launched for the Mediterranean service in 1860. Lengthened and fitted with compound engines in 1873 for the Atlantic which she briefly served before returning to the Mediterranean run. Scrapped in 1896.

Aurania

Gross tonnage 7,269
Dimensions - m 143.3 x 17.4
Builder J & G Thomson, Glasgow
Maiden voyage 1883
Career Had greater breadth to length ratio for comfort and stability. When engines failed mid-Atlantic, towed under sail into port by three tugs. Carried 30,000 troops to Boer War and Hungarian immigrants to America from Trieste. Scrapped in 1905.

Aurania II

Gross tonnage 13,936
Dimensions - m 158.6 x 19.5
Builder Swan Hunter, Newcastle
Maiden voyage 1917
Career Immediately recruited as a troop transport and sank after torpedo hit in 1918 with loss of nine crew.

Aurania III

Gross tonnage 13,984
Dimensions - m 158.4 x 19.9
Builder Swan Hunter, Newcastle
Maiden voyage 1924
Career Served on New York and Montreal services.
When a convoy escort in WW2, survived collision
with an iceberg and torpedo hit in 1941. Sold for
conversion to fleet repair ship, 1942. Broken up in 1961.

Ausonia

Gross tonnage 7,907
Dimensions - m 137.3 x 16.5
Builder Swan Hunter, Newcastle
Maiden voyage 1911
Career Launched 1909 for Thomson Line and bought
in 1911 as one of three Cunarders to inaugurate
Southampton-Montreal service. After being
torpedoed and shelled in 1918, sank, all but 44 crew
escaping in five lifeboats.

Ausonia II

Gross tonnage 13,912
Dimensions - m 158.5 x 19.9
Builder Armstrong Whitworth, Newcastle
Maiden voyage 1922
Career Called at Hamburg as part of Canadian
emigrant route. Served as Atlantic convoy during
WW2. In 1944 sold and converted to fleet repair
ship for the Burma and Japanese campaigns.
Scrapped in 1965.

Australasian

Gross tonnage 2,902
Dimensions - m 101.1 x 12.8
Builder J & G Thomson Glasgow
Maiden voyage 1860
Career Bought by Cunard in 1859 who retained her
unwieldy name until 1870 when renamed Calabria
after refit to accommodate 900 emigrants. Sold in
1876, ending days as a telegraph cable laying ship.
Scrapped in 1898.

Balbec

Gross tonnage 774
Dimensions - m 63.8 x 9.2
Builder William Denny & Bros, Dumbarton
Maiden voyage 1853
Career Served on both the Medierranean and Atlantic
routes before fatally striking a sunken wreck in the
English Channel in 1884.

Batavia

Gross tonnage 2,553
Dimensions - m 99.8 x 12
Builder William Denny & Bros, Dumbarton
Maiden voyage 1870
Career In 1880 made trial run to Bombay, Cunard's
only venture into the Eastern trade. In 1882
transported troops to Egypt. Sold to Canadian Pacific
in 1887. Seized, 1905 for conveying contraband
during Russo-Japanese War. Scrapped in 1924.

Berengaria

Gross tonnage 52,226
Dimensions - m 269 x 30
Builder A G Vulcan, Hamburg
Maiden voyage 1919
Career Built as the Imperator for the Hamburg-America Line in 1911 but seized and given to Cunard at end of WW1. Following two fires attributed to faulty wiring, retired in 1938 although hull not finally dismantled until 1946.

Bothnia

Gross tonnage 4,535
Dimensions - m 128.7 x 12.9
Builder J & G Thomson, Glasgow
Maiden voyage 1874
Career Sister to the Scythia, plied the New York and Boston routes until sold in 1896. Scrapped in 1899.

Britannia

Gross tonnage 1,135
Dimensions - m 63.1 x 10.4
Builder Robert Duncan, Greenock
Maiden voyage 1840
Career The first Cunarder of all. Sold in 1848 to the German navy and sunk when being used as target practice in 1880.

Britannic III

Gross tonnage 26,943
Dimensions - m 208.4 x 25.1
Builder Harland & Wolff, Belfast
Maiden voyage 1935
Career Acquired with Cunard-White Star merger, 1934. Served on London, Southampton, Le Havre, New York route. Carried 180,000 troops during WW2. From 1950 sailed on the Liverpool-New York route. Scrapped in 1960.

British Queen

Gross tonnage 772
Dimensions - m 59.4 x 8.8
Builder William Denny & Bros, Dumbarton
Maiden voyage 1851
Career This modest vessel was Cunard's first Queen. Trialled the Mediterranean service. Served as transport in Crimean War. When larger ships replaced her, served the Liverpool-Le Havre feeder route. Scrapped in 1899.

Calabria   See Australasian

Caledonia

Gross tonnage 1,138
Dimensions - m 63.1 x 10.4
Builder R Wood, Port Glasgow
Maiden voyage 1840
Career One of the original four Cunarders. Sold to the Spanish navy in 1850 and wrecked off Havana the next year.

California

Gross tonnage 8,662
Dimensions - m 143.3 x 17.7
Builder D & W Henderson Ltd, Glasgow
Maiden voyage 1907
Career Launched in partnership with the Anchor Line, torpedoed in 1917 off Ireland and sank in seven minutes. The Captain went down with the ship but was blown to the surface by an explosion and survived.

Cambria

Gross tonnage 1,423
Dimensions - m 66.7 x 10.7
Builder Robert Steele & Son, Greenock
Maiden voyage 1844
Career One of two larger Cunarders commissioned to meet increased demand. From 1848 alternated between New York and Boston. Sold to Garibaldi in 1860, joining the Italian navy until scrapped in 1875.

Cameronia

Gross tonnage 10,963
Dimensions - m 157.0 x 19.0
Builder D & W Henderson Ltd, Glasgow
Maiden voyage 1915
Career Originally built for the Anchor Line, joined the joint Anchor-Cunard service in 1915. Torpedoed in 1917 while carrying 2,650 troops from Marseilles to Alexandria.

Cameronia II

Gross tonnage 16,280
Dimensions - m 176.3 x 21.4
Builder William Beardmore and Co, Clydebank
Maiden voyage 1921
Career Served Cunard/Anchor route to New York. Refitted in 1928 to correct tendency to roll. Sold 1935. After trooping duties in WW2, became one-class emigrant ship for Australia. Scrapped in 1957.

Campania

Gross tonnage 12,950
Dimensions - m 183.2 x 19.9
Builder Fairfield Shipbuilding, Glasgow
Maiden voyage 1893
Career Broke the Atlantic speed record in both directions. First Cunarder fitted with a Marconi wireless telegraph. As seaplane carrier in WWI, first ship to launch aircraft while under way. Sank after collision in port four days before the end of WWI.

Canada

Gross tonnage 1,831
Dimensions - m 76.5 x 11.6
Builder Robert Steele & Co, Greenock
Maiden voyage 1848
Career One of the Cunarders that doubled the fleet after the Admiralty contract of 1847. Served both New York and Boston surviving several accidents. Sold and converted to sailing ship Mississippi in 1867 and scrapped in 1883.

Carinthia II

Gross tonnage 20,277
Dimensions - m 183.1 x 22.5
Builder Vickers Ltd, Barrow
Maiden voyage 1925
Career One of the first Cunarders designed for winter cruising from New York while returning to the Atlantic run in summer. Served as armed merchant cruiser in WW2 until torpedoed and sunk in the Mediterranean in 1940.

Carinthia III

Gross tonnage 21,947
Dimensions - m 173.7 x 24.5
Builder John Brown's, Clydebank
Maiden voyage 1956
Career Serving the Canadian run, her career was plagued by collisions, fires and strikes. She was the last of the four Cunarders left on this route before being sold to a series of cruise lines from 1968.

Carmania

Gross tonnage 19,524
Dimensions - m 198.2 x 22.0
Builder John Brown's, Clydebank
Maiden voyage 1905
Career In 1913 rescued survivors from blazing emigrant ship Volturno in mid-Atlantic. In 1914 sank the German Cap Trafalgar. Assisted in Gallipoli Landings and in quelling a British mutiny. Cruised during 1920s. Scrapped in1931.

Carmania II   See Saxonia

Caronia

Gross tonnage 19,687
Dimensions - m 198.1 x 22.0
Builder John Brown's, Clydebank
Maiden voyage 1905
Career The 'pretty sister' whose wartime activities included contraband patrols off New York and repatriating Canadian troops. In 1919 inaugurated London-Canada service. Scrapped in 1933.

Caronia II

Gross tonnage 34,183
Dimensions - m 209.6 x 27.9
Builder John Brown's, Clydebank
Maiden voyage 1949
Career World's first purpose-built cruise ship. On first cruise in 1951, called at 30 ports. Took Americans to the Queen's coronation in 1953. Sold in 1967 and after chequered career sank on way to breaker's yard in 1974.

Caronia III

Gross tonnage 24,492
Dimensions - m 191.0 x 25.0
Builder Swan Hunter, Newcastle
Maiden voyage 1983
Career Built as Vistafjord for Norwegian American Line, 1973. Bought by Cunard Line, 1983. Renamed and reflagged to Great Britain in 1999. Sold to Saga in 2004.

Carpathia

Gross tonnage 13,555
Dimensions - m 164.6 x 19.7
Builder Swan Hunter, Newcastle
Maiden voyage 1903
Career Designed for the Hungarian emigrant service from Fiume. In 1912, mercy dash to save survivors from the Titanic. Continued in commercial service throughout WWI. Sunk by three torpedoes in 1918.

Cassandra

Gross tonnage 8,135
Dimensions - m 138.7 x 16.2
Builder Scott's of Greenock
Maiden voyage 1924
Career Chartered 1924-6 from Donaldson Line for the Canadian route. Served as cargo vessel until sold to a German shipping line in 1929. Scrapped in 1934.

Catalonia

Gross tonnage 4,481
Dimensions - m 130.9 x 13.1
Builder J & G Thomson, Glasgow
Maiden voyage 1881
Career Served initially on the New York and then the Boston route. Carried troops to Egypt in 1882 and to the Boer War after which she was scrapped in 1901.

Cephalonia

Gross tonnage 5,517
Dimensions - m 131.2 x 14.2
Builder Laird Bros, Birkenhead
Maiden voyage 1882
Career Largest merchant ship built on the Mersey to that time, First Cunarder fitted with refrigeration chambers. After trooping in the Boer War sold to Chinese Eastern Railway Co. Sunk in 1904 during Russo-Japanese War.

China

Gross tonnage 2,638
Dimensions - m 99.4 x 12.3
Builder Robert Napier and Sons
Maiden voyage 1862
Career First Cunarder with accommodation for emigrants. Sold to Spain in 1880. Lost at sea while sailing as a four masted barque in 1906.

Columbia

Gross tonnage 1,175
Dimensions - m 63.1 x 10.4
Builder Robert Steele & Son, Greenock
Maiden voyage 1841
Career One of the first four Cunarders. Wrecked in 1843 off the coast of Nova Scotia although passengers, crew and the mail were rescued.

Crown Dynasty

Gross tonnage 19,089
Dimensions - m 163.8 x 22.5
Builder Wärtsilä, Helsinki
Maiden voyage 1994
Career Taken over by Cunard from Commodore Cruise Line. The deal increased the Cunard fleet to ten ships and over 7,000 berths. Sold in 1997 and renamed Braemar by a later owner.

Crown Jewel

Gross tonnage 19,089
Dimensions - m 163.8 x 22.5
Builder Union Naval de Levante, Valencia
Maiden voyage 1993
Career Sister cruiser of the Crown Dynasty. Sold to Star Cruises in 1995 and renamed SuperStar Gemini.

Crown Monarch

Gross tonnage 19,089
Dimensions - m 163.8 x 22.5
Builder Union Naval de Levante, Valencia
Maiden voyage 1993
Career Built for Commodore Line, Cunard ran her as a cruise ship in 1993-4. After several changes in ownership now runs gambling cruises from Hong Kong under the name MV Walrus.

Cuba

Gross tonnage 2,668
Dimensions - m 103.1 x 12.9
Builder Tod & McGregor, Glasgow
Maiden voyage 1864
Career Served the Liverpool-New York route. In 1876 sold and converted into sailing ship. In 1887 wrecked on voyage from Calcutta to Hull.

Cunard Adventurer

Gross tonnage 14,110
Dimensions - m 147.5 x 21.5m
Builder Rotterdamsche Droogdok, Rotterdam
Maiden voyage 1971
Career The 806 passenger cruise liner was originally commissioned by an airline before Cunard took her over during construction. Sold to Norwegian Caribbean Line in 1977.

Cunard Ambassador

Gross tonnage 14,151
Dimensions - m 147.5 x 21.5
Builder Rotterdamsche Droogdok, Rotterdam
Maiden voyage 1972
Career After an engine room fire in 1974 sold for conversion as a livestock carrier. Scrapped in 1984.

Cunard Countess

Gross tonnage 7,495
Dimensions - m 163.0 x 22.8
Builder Burmeister Wain Skilos, Copenhagen
Maiden voyage 1976
Career Christened by Mrs Neil Armstrong, the wife of the first person to walk on the moon. Originally had white funnel. Served as trooper during Falkland conflict. Sold in 1996: later owned by Indonesian and Greek cruise lines.

Cunard Princess

Gross tonnage 17,495
Dimensions - m 163.0 x 22.8
Builder Burmeister Wain Skilos, Copenhagen
Maiden voyage 1977
Career Originally named Conquest until rejected as too aggressive. Served as respite centre for US troops during Gulf War, 1991. Sold in 1995 to Italian cruise line and renamed Rhapsody.

Czar

Gross tonnage 6,503
Dimensions - m 129.6 x 16.2
Builder Barclay, Curle & Co, Glasgow, Scotland
Maiden voyage 1917
Career Built in 1912 for Russian American Line. Seized by the Allies in 1917 and used by Cunard. Sold in 1921 to the America Baltic Line.

Damascus

Gross tonnage 1,213
Dimensions - m 77.1 x 9.6
Builder William Denny & Bros, Dumbarton
Maiden voyage 1856
Career Switching from Mediterranean to North Atlantic route in 1860. Acquired by the shipbuilder in part payment for the Morocco, 1861. Went through several changes of ownership before being scrapped in 1912.

Emeu

Gross tonnage 1,358
Dimensions - m 81.7 x 11.2
Builder Robert Napier & Sons, Glasgow
Maiden voyage 1854
Career Bought by Cunard in 1854 to ease the strain of having so many ships on active duty during the Crimean War. Sold in 1857, later joining the P & O fleet. Wrecked in 1880.

Etna

Gross tonnage 2,215
Dimensions - m 93 x 11.5
Builder Caird & Co, Greenock
Maiden voyage 1855
Career Immediately requisitioned as Crimean troop ship. Later hired out to a number of lines before being sold in 1881 to Italian shipping line which renamed her three times in the next three years. Scrapped in 1896.

Etruria

Gross tonnage 7,718
Dimensions - m 93.0 x 11.5
Builder John Elder & Co, Glasgow
Maiden voyage 1885
Career One of two largest ships of her day. Sailed uneventfully on Liverpool-New York run until series of mid-ocean breakdowns, an encounter with a freak wave and collisions in early 1900s. Scrapped in 1910 after collision prevented her last crossing.

Europa

Gross tonnage 1,834
Dimensions - m 76.5 x 11.6
Builder John Wood, Port Glasgow
Maiden voyage 1848
Career One of four paddle steamers built to double the fleet. In 1849 collided with emigrant ship Charles Bartlett which sank with the loss of 135 lives and in 1858 collided with a fellow Cunarder Arabia damaging both. Sold in 1867.

Feltria

Gross tonnage 5,254
Dimensions - m 128 x 14.7
Builder William Denny & Bros, Dumbarton
Maiden voyage 1916
Career Built in 1891. Served several owners including acting as the royal yacht for the visit of the King and Queen of Denmark to Greenland. Bought by Cunard in 1916. Torpedoed off Ireland with loss of 45 lives in 1917.

Flavia

Gross tonnage 9,285
Dimensions - m 143.3 x 17.3
Builder Palmers Co Ltd, Jarrow
Maiden voyage 1916
Career Launched in 1901. After several owners Cunard bought her in 1916 to make up for war losses. Sailed on Avonmouth-Canada route. In 1918 torpedoed and sank off Ireland.

Franconia

Gross tonnage 18,150
Dimensions - m 183.0 x 21.7
Builder Swan Hunter, Newcastle
Maiden voyage 1911
Career Alternated between the North Atlantic and Mediterranean cruising until 1913 when requisitioned as a 2,700 capacity troop ship for the Gallipoli campaign. Torpedoed and sunk in Mediterranean in 1916.

Franconia II

Gross tonnage 20,158
Dimensions - m 183.3 x 22.5
Builder John Brown's, Clydebank
Maiden voyage 1923
Career Spent winters cruising and summers on New York run. During WW2 carried over 189,000 troops including evacuation from France and North Africa landings. In 1945 Churchill's base at the Yalta Conference. Resumed passenger service to Canada. Scrapped in 1956.

Franconia III   See Ivernia II

Gallia

Gross tonnage 4,809
Dimensions - m 131.1 x 13.6
Builder J & G Thomson, Glasgow
Maiden voyage 1879
Career Served on the New York and Boston routes with accommodation for 1,200 third class passengers. Crossed the Atlantic in seven days in 1886. Sold in 1897 and scrapped three years later.

Georgic

Gross tonnage 27,759
Dimensions - m 208.4 x 25.1
Builder Harland and Wolff, Belfast
Maiden voyage 1934
Career Last ship to be launched for the White Star Line, Cunard acquiring her on merger in 1934. Largest ship to sail out of London. In 1941, when trooping, bombed, sunk but salvaged in Gulf of Suez. Trooper in Korean War. Scrapped in 1956.

Hecla

Gross tonnage 1,785
Dimensions - m 84.1 x 11.1
Builder Robert Napier & Sons, Glasgow
Maiden voyage 1860
Career Sailed mainly on the Liverpool-Boston route until sold in 1881. Five names later she became a hulk in 1924 after a collision. Scrapped in 1954 making her one of the longest lived Cunard-built ships.

Hibernia

Gross tonnage 1,422
Dimensions - m 66.7 x 10.7
Builder Robert Steele & Co, Greenock
Maiden voyage 1843
Career With the Cambria, supplemented Cunard's first fleet to meet increased mail and passenger demand. Sold to the Spanish navy in 1850. Lost in 1868.

Homeric

Gross tonnage 34,352
Dimensions - m 228.9 x 25.4
Builder F Schichau, Danzig
Maiden voyage 1935
Career The half-built German liner given to White Star at the end of WWI and passed to Cunard-White Star in 1934. Largest double screw vessel in service: popular with public as very stable in rough seas. Scrapped during Depression.

Ivernia

Gross tonnage 14,058
Dimensions - m 177.4 x 19.8
Builder Swan Hunter, Newcastle
Maiden voyage 1900
Career The largest cargo vessel of her day, also capable of carrying over 1,950 passengers. Served Boston route. When acting as WWI trooper, torpedoed and sunk off Greece in 1916 with 36 crew and 84 troops lost.

Ivernia II

Gross tonnage 17,707
Dimensions - m 182.4 x 24.2
Builder John Brown's, Clydebank
Maiden voyage 1955
Career Initially served the Canadian route. Renamed Franconia in 1963 when rebuilt for cruising. Sold in 1973 to the Soviet Union as a cruise ship and named after the Russian opera star Feodor Shalyapin.

Java

Gross tonnage 2,696
Dimensions - m 102.7 x 13.1
Builder J & G Thomson, Glasgow
Maiden voyage 1865
Career Uneventful career on the Boston and New York routes. Sold in 1878 to the Red Star Line. Went missing en route from San Francisco to Queenstown in 1895.

Jura

Gross tonnage 2,241
Dimensions - m 95.7 x 11.0
Builder J & G Thomson, Glasgow
Maiden voyage 1857
Career Immediately requisitioned for Crimean War. Maiden voyage to Alexandria on charter to another line. Served on New York and Montreal routes until early 1860s when sold to Allan Line. Wrecked off Liverpool in 1864.

Karnak

Gross tonnage 1,116
Dimensions - m 68.52 x 11.15
Builder William Denny & Bros, Dumbarton
Maiden voyage 1855
Career Launched in 1853 but immediately requisitioned for the Crimean War. Returned to the Mediterranean service in 1855. Wrecked near Alexandria in 1862.

Kedar

Gross tonnage 1,863
Dimensions - m 84.1 x 11.0
Builder William Denny & Bros, Dumbarton
Maiden voyage 1860
Career After a brief period on the Atlantic spent most of career on the Mediterranean service. Sold for scrap in 1897.

Laconia

Gross tonnage 18,099
Dimensions - m 183 x 21.7
Builder Swan Hunter, Newcastle
Maiden voyage 1912
Career With sister Franconia carried emigrants from southern Europe and stood in on Atlantic run for the Mauretania and Lusitania when being refitted. Converted to armed cruiser, serving in South Atlantic and Indian Oceans, before being torpedoed off Ireland in 1917.

Laconia II

Gross tonnage 19,860
Dimensions - m 183.3 x 22.5
Builder Swan Hunter, Newcastle
Maiden voyage 1921
Career Made world's first cruise in 1922, calling at 22 ports. After serving New York run, returned to cruising in 1935. In 1942, laden with Italian POWs, hit by torpedo in South Atlantic: survivors rescued by U-boats which cut lifeboats loose when bombed by American plane.

Lancastria

Gross tonnage 16,243
Dimensions - m 168.5 x 21.4
Builder William Beardmore & Co Ltd, Clydebank
Maiden voyage 1922
Career Commissioned for the Allan Line as the Tyrrhenia: Cunard changed her unpopular name on acquiring her. Served largely as cruise ship until WW2. Bombed in St Nazaire harbour in 1940 in worst tragedy in British maritime history. Site now an official War Grave.

Laurentic

Gross tonnage 18,724
Dimensions - m 176.2 x 23.0
Builder Harland & Wolff, Belfast
Maiden voyage 1934
Career Built for White Star Line in 1927. Last major Atlantic liner with coal fired, triple expansion engines. After collision in 1935, laid up apart from trooping to Palestine, 1936. Sunk in 1940: Hitler decorated the U-boat commander with equivalent of Victoria Cross.

Lebanon

Gross tonnage 1,373
Dimensions - m 76.8 x 9.1
Builder J & G Thomson, Glasgow
Maiden voyage 1855
Career Acquired by Cunard a year after its maiden voyage as the Aerolith the previous year. In 1857 served as a trooper during the Indian mutiny. Sold to the Spanish government in 1859.

Letitia

Gross tonnage 13,475
Dimensions - m 164 x 20.2
Builder Fairfield's, Glasgow
Maiden voyage 1925
Career Chartered by Cunard from Anchor-Donaldson Line in which it had a financial interest. After war duty as a troop transport and Canadian hospital ship, refitted as an Australian and Canadian emigrant ship, Captain Cook for Donaldson Line. Scrapped in 1960.

Lucania

Gross tonnage 12,952
Dimensions - m 183.2 x 19.9
Builder Fairfield Shipbuilding, Glasgow
Maiden voyage 1893
Career Enormous by the standards of the day. Won Blue Riband on maiden voyage and renowned for speed and reliability on New York route. Broken up after serious fire when in Liverpool in 1909.

Lusitania

Gross tonnage 31,550
Dimensions - m 232.3 x 26.8
Builder John Brown's, Clydebank
Maiden voyage 1907
Career One of two superliners built with Government assistance to win back the Blue Riband for Britain. Largest vessel afloat of her day. Torpedoed and sunk off Ireland in 1915 with the loss of 1,200 lives. The sinking helped to bring America into the war.

Majestic

Gross tonnage 56,551
Dimensions - m 279.0 x 30.5
Builder Blohm & Voss, Hamburg
Maiden voyage 1934
Career Built for Hamburg-America Line as the Bismarck, the world's largest ship. As Cunard-White Star liner, replaced the Mauretania on the New York crossing from 1934 until replaced by the Queen Mary in 1936. Sold as cadet training ship: caught fire in 1939 and scrapped.

Malta

Gross tonnage 2,132
Dimensions - m 92.4 x 12.0
Builder J & G Thomson, Glasgow
Maiden voyage 1866
Career Served on New York, Boston and Mediterranean runs. In 1889 wrecked in fog off Land's End without loss of life.

Marathon

Gross tonnage 1,784
Dimensions - m 84.1 x 11.1
Builder Robert Napier & Sons, Glasgow
Maiden voyage 1861
Career Sailed Liverpool-New York until 1873 and then on Boston route. Served in the Egyptian campaign in 1882. Served the Liverpool-Mediterranean route from 1884 until scrapped in 1889.

Mauretania

Gross tonnage 31,938
Dimensions - m 232.3 x 26.8
Builder Swan, Hunter, Newcastle
Maiden voyage 1907
Career One of Cunard's most successful liners. Blue Riband holder for over 20 years. During WWI served as a hospital ship and carried troops to Gallipoli and across the Atlantic. Returned to Atlantic service and later cruising. Scrapped in 1935.

Mauretania II

Gross tonnage 35,738
Dimensions - m 225.4 x 27.2
Builder Cammell, Laird, Birkenhead
Maiden voyage 1939
Career Made five Atlantic crossings before being requisitioned, carrying troops from Australia and North America. Returned in 1947 to Atlantic crossings in the summer and cruises in the winter. Painted green in 1962 as cruise ship. Scrapped in 1965.

Media

Gross tonnage 13,345
Dimensions - m 181.8 x 21.4
Builder John Brown's, Clydebank
Maiden voyage 1947
Career Built as a combination passenger-cargo ship for Cunard. Sold to an Italian Line in 1961 and subsequently converted to a cruise ship before being scrapped in 1989 after a fire in Hong Kong harbour.

Melita

Gross tonnage 1,254
Dimensions - m 71.0 x 8.8
Builder Alexander Denny, Dumbarton
Maiden voyage 1853
Career Built for the Cunard Mediterranean service, transferred to Atlantic in 1860 before being sold back to its builders in 1861. Destroyed by fire at sea in 1868.

Nemesis

Gross tonnage 2,717
Dimensions - m 107.5 x 12.6
Builder Tod & McGregor, Glasgow
Maiden voyage 1869
Career Launched for P & O as Delphi. Bought by Cunard in 1869 and sailed Liverpool-New York until 1870. Contracted out to other lines before being sold to Belgian Red Star Line in 1869. Scrapped in 1891.

Niagara

Gross tonnage 1,824
Dimensions - m 76.5 x 11.6
Builder Robert Steele & Co., Greenock
Maiden voyage 1848
Career Sailed on the Atlantic mail service until 1855 when contracted as troop transport in the Crimean War. After serving Liverpool-Le Havre route, sold in 1866. Wrecked off Wales in 1875.

Olympic

Gross tonnage 45,342
Dimensions - m 259.8 x 28.2
Builder Harland & Wolff, Belfast
Maiden voyage 1934
Career Launched in 1911 for White Star and taken over by Cunard in 1934. On maiden voyage with Cunard, collided with the Nantucket lightship in fog, killing eight people. Sold in 1935 and scrapped two years later.

Olympus

Gross tonnage 1,794
Dimensions - m 84.1 x 11.2
Builder J & G Thomson, Glasgow
Maiden voyage 1860
Career Built for the Mediterranean service. In 1872 enlarged to 2,425 tonnes, thereafter sailing on the Liverpool-Boston run before being sold to its makers in 1881 Scrapped in 1891.

Orduna

Gross tonnage 15,499
Dimensions - m 167.7 x 20.5
Builder Harland & Wolff, Belfast
Maiden voyage 1914
Career Built for the Pacific Steam Navigation Co in 1913 but chartered by Cunard 1914-1920 sailing between Liverpool and New York. Returned to its owners, not scrapped until 1951.

Oregon

Gross tonnage 7,324
Dimensions - m 152.7 x 16.5
Builder John Elder & Co., Glasgow
Maiden voyage 1884
Career Launched for the Guion Line but immediately bought by Cunard for Atlantic service. Requisitioned briefly in late 1884 during war scare with Russia. In 1886 collided with an unidentified schooner and sank off Long Island.

Palestine

Gross tonnage 1,800
Dimensions - m 84.1 x 11.0
Builder Robert Steele & Co., Greenock
Maiden voyage 1860
Career Although built for Cunard first served for the Allan Line before serving on the Atlantic for Cunard from 1860. Sold in 1872. Enlarged and sailed for the Dominion and Warren Lines. Scrapped in 1896.

Palmyra

Gross tonnage 2,044
Dimensions - m 88.6 x 11.6
Builder Caird & Co., Greenock
Maiden voyage 1866
Career Sailed the Atlantic from Liverpool until 1873 and then mainly from the Mediterranean. Served as a transport ship in Zulu war, 1880-1 and 1882 Egyptian campaign. Scrapped in 1896.

Pannonia

Gross tonnage 9,851
Dimensions - m 148.3 x 18.1
Builder John Brown's, Clydebank
Maiden voyage 1904
Career Carried mainly emigrants from Fiume, Trieste and Palermo to New York until 1914. During WWI carried Canadian troops to France. Returned to Mediterranean service 1919-1921. Scrapped in 1922.

Parthia

Gross tonnage 3,167
Dimensions - m 109.9 x 12.3
Builder William Denny & Bros, Dumbarton
Maiden voyage 1870
Career Sailed on Liverpool-New York route. Served as a troopship for 1881 Egyptian campaign. Sold in 1883. Varied career included inaugurating cruising in Alaska as the Victoria in 1934 before being scrapped in 1956.

Parthia II

Gross tonnage 13,362
Dimensions - m 160.4 x 21.4
Builder Harland & Wolff, Belfast
Maiden voyage 1948
Career Sailed Liverpool-New York route. In 1950 received the ship's bell from Parthia I. Sold in 1963 to P&O, renamed Remuera and served London-New Zealand run. Scrapped in 1969.

Pavonia

Gross tonnage 5,588
Dimensions - m 131.2 x 14.1
Builder J&G Thomson, Glasgow
Maiden voyage 1882
Career Sailed mainly between Liverpool and Boston. Broke down in the Azores in 1899 and had to be towed back to Liverpool. After service in the Boer War, sold and scrapped in 1900.

Persia

Gross tonnage 3,300
Dimensions - m 114.6 x 13.7
Builder Robert Napier & Sons, Glasgow
Maiden voyage 1856
Career The largest liner in the world at the time of her launch, the Persia was Cunard's first iron ship. She sailed Liverpool-New York until 1867, being scapped five years later.

Prinses Irene

Gross tonnage 8,533
Dimensions - m 138.1 x 19.0
Builder De Merwede van Vliet & Co, Netherlands
Maiden voyage 1964
Career Passenger-cargo ship launched in 1959 for Oranje Line, Holland. Bought in 1964 for Cunard Brocklebank Great Lakes service. Sold in 1965 to Indonesia. Scrapped in 1983.

Queen Elizabeth

Gross tonnage 83,673
Dimensions - m 300.9 x 36.1
Builder John Brown & Co, Glasgow
Maiden voyage 1940
Career Painted grey and left secretly for New York on outbreak of WW2. Made 64 crossings as a troop carrier. Returned to passenger service, 1946 and started cruising in 1962. Sold in 1968. Burnt out in Hong Kong while being converted to a floating University.

Queen Elizabeth 2

Gross tonnage 70,327
Dimensions - m 293.5 x 32.1
Builder Upper Clyde Shipbuilders, Glasgow
Maiden voyage 1969
Career Throughout her career has mixed Atlantic crossings with cruising. Served as a troop carrier during the Falklands War in 1982. Made final trans-Atlantic crossing, 2004, accompanied by QM2, the new Cunard Line flagship.

By 1996 Cunard invested more than 10 times the building cost of QE2, including a massive re-engineering in Nov 1986-April 1987 which involved fitting nine diesel electric engines, new propellers and equipment to capture heat expelled by the engines, and a major interior redesign in 1994. Since then a further upgrading at Southampton in 1996 involved 1,000 workers. In 1999 following acquisition by Carnival the QE2 underwent a further refurbishment. In 1996, QE2's transatlantic crossing time was extended from five to six days.

Queen Mary

Gross tonnage 80,774
Dimensions - m 297.2 x 36.1
Builder John Brown's, Clydebank
Maiden voyage 1936
Career On Atlantic service until WW2 when served as a troopship helping to win the Battle of the Atlantic. Returned to Atlantic service in 1947 after ferrying war brides to North America. In 1963 started cruising. Sold to Long Beach, California as a museum and hotel in 1967.

Queen Mary 2

Gross tonnage 150,000
Dimensions - m 345.0 x 41.0
Builder ALSTOM Chantiers de l'Atlantique
Maiden voyage 2004
Career As high as a 23-storey building and longer than the Eiffel Tower is tall, QM2 is the largest, tallest, longest, broadest and most expensive ocean liner ever built. Named by the Queen, she will pass the QE2 on her final Atlantic voyage as she becomes Cunard Line's flagship.

Royal George

Gross tonnage 11,146
Dimensions - m 160.3 x 18.3
Builder Fairfield Shipbuilding, Glasgow
Maiden voyage 1919
Career Launched in 1907 as the Heliopolis. Bought and renamed Royal George by Canadian Northern Steamships, taken over by Cunard during WWI. Sailed the Atlantic 1919-1920. Scrapped in 1922.

Royal Viking Sun

Gross tonnage 37,845
Dimensions - m 205.5 x 28.9
Builder Wartsila, Finland
Maiden voyage 1994
Career Cruise liner launched in 1988 for Royal Viking Line. Bought by Cunard in 1994 and sold in 1999 to Seabourn Cruise Line. Resold in 2002 to Holland America Line and renamed Prinsendam 2.

Russia

Gross tonnage 2,960
Dimensions - m 109.1 x 13.1
Builder J &G Thomson, Glasgow
Maiden voyage 1867
Career Earned reputation for speed and comfort on the Liverpool-New York route. Sold to Red Funnel Line in 1880 and renamed Waesland. After being sold again and renamed Philadelphia, sank after a collision off Wales in 1902.

Sagafjord

Gross tonnage 20,147
Dimensions - m 188.0 x 24.5
Builder Soc des Forges de la Mediterranee, France
Maiden voyage 1983
Career Built in 1965 for Norwegian American Line and bought by Cunard in 1983. Chartered in 1996 and sold in 1997 being renamed Saga Rose.

Samaria

Gross tonnage 2,574
Dimensions - m 97.7 x 12.0
Builder J & G Thomson, Glasgow
Maiden voyage 1869
Career Worked the Atlantic route first to New York, then to Boston. Refitted in 1878, and withdrawn in 1896 before being sold to an Italian line in 1902 and later scrapped.

Samaria II

Gross tonnage 19,602
Dimensions - m 183.3 x 22.5
Builder Cammell Laird, Birkenhead
Maiden voyage 1922
Career Combined the Liverpool-New York and Boston runs with cruising from 1923. Collided with the Aquitania in the blackout, 1939. War service carrying troops, evacuees and refugees. Returned to Atlantic crossings until 1955 when scrapped.

Saragossa

Gross tonnage 2,263
Dimensions - m 96.40 x 10.76m
Builder J & G Thomson, Glasgow
Maiden voyage 1874
Career Made only one trans-Atlantic crossing before plying from Liverpool to the Mediterranean. Sold to Italian line in 1880. Scrapped in1909.

Saxonia

Gross tonnage 14,281
Dimensions - m 176.8 x 19.8
Builder John Brown's, Clydebank
Maiden voyage 1900
Career Sailed Liverpool-Boston until 1911 when switched to carrying emigrants to New York from Trieste and Fiume. Requisitioned as a troopship in 1917. Resumed Atlantic crossings before being scrapped in 1925.

Saxonia II

Gross tonnage 21,637
Dimensions - m 173.7 x 24.5
Builder John Brown's, Clydebank
Maiden voyage 1954
Career The first of four ships built for the Montreal route. With declining traffic, refitted in 1963 for cruising and renamed the Carmania. After running aground near the Bahamas in 1969 laid up and later sold to the USSR.

Scotia

Gross tonnage 3,817
Dimensions - m 115.6 x 14.7
Builder Robert Napier and Sons, Glasgow
Maiden voyage 1862
Career Admired as the finest ship in the world of its day. She was Cunard's last iron paddle steamer. Sold in 1879. Wrecked in 1904 after second career as cable laying ship.

Scythia

Gross tonnage 4,557
Dimensions - m 128.2 x 12.9
Builder J & G Thomson, Glasgow
Maiden voyage 1875
Career Sailed Liverpool-New York and Boston routes. In 1875 broke a propeller blade after colliding with a whale, having to return under sail. In 1881 rescued the crew of the schooner Mary. Sold for scrap in 1898.

Scythia II

Gross tonnage 19,730
Dimensions - m 183.1 x 22.5
Builder Vickers Ltd., Barrow
Maiden voyage 1921
Career Switched between cruising and the Atlantic run. Carried troops and evacuated children to North America in WW2. Survived a torpedo strike in Algiers harbour. Returned to Cunard before being sold for scrap in 1958.

Sea Goddess

Gross tonnage 4,253
Dimensions - m 104.8 x 14.6
Builder Wartsila, Finland
Maiden voyage 1986
Career Built in 1984 for Sea Goddess Cruises which was taken over by Cunard. Sold in 2001 and renamed Sea Dream.

Sea Goddess II

Gross tonnage 4,253
Dimensions - m 104.8 x 14.6
Builder Hollming Oy, Finland
Maiden voyage 1986
Career Built in 1985 for Sea Goddess Cruises which was taken over by Cunard. Sold in 2001 and renamed Sea Dream II.

Servia

Gross tonnage 7,392
Dimensions - m 157.0 x 15.9
Builder J & G Thomson, Glasgow
Maiden voyage 1881
Career The first steel Cunarder, sailed on the Liverpool-New York route. Requistioned in 1899 as a troop ship for the Boer War. Scrapped in 1902.

Siberia

Gross tonnage 2,498
Dimensions - m 97.5 x 11.9
Builder J & G Thomson, Glasgow
Maiden voyage 1867
Career Sister ship of the Samaria. Sailed on Liverpool–New York and Boston routes. Sold in 1880 to shipyard in part payment for the Catalonia. Sold and renamed Manila. Wrecked in 1882.

Sidon

Gross tonnage 1,872
Dimensions - m 84.0 x 11.0
Builder William Denny & Co, Dumbarton
Maiden voyage 1863
Career Served on Mediterranean and Atlantic routes. Wrecked off Spanish coast in 1885.

Slavonia

Gross tonnage 10,606
Dimensions - m 155.4 x 18.1
Builder Sir J Laing & Sons, Sunderland
Maiden voyage 1904
Career Launched in 1902 for the British India Line. Sold to Cunard as proved too big. Sailed as emigrant ship from Fiume, Trieste and Palermo to New York. Broke up in 1909 when ran onto rocks in fog in the Azores. All passengers rescued.

Sylvania

Gross tonnage 5,598
Dimensions - m 135.6 x 14.9
Builder London & Glasgow Co, Glasgow
Maiden voyage 1895
Career One of Cunard's Atlantic cargo vessels. Requisitioned in 1900 to carry mules from New Orleans to Cape Town for the Boer War. Sold to an Italian company in 1910.

Sylvania II

Gross tonnage 21,989
Dimensions - m 173.7 x 24.5
Builder John Brown's, Clydebank
Maiden voyage 1957
Career The last of four ships built for the Liverpool-Montreal route which she served until 1960 before switching to Halifax and New York until 1966. Sold in 1968 to Italian Sitmar line who renamed her Fairwind and operated her as a cruise liner. Scrapped in 2004.

Tarifa

Gross tonnage 2,058
Dimensions - m 89.1 x 11.6
Builder J & G Thomson, Glasgow
Maiden voyage 1865
Career Sailed on the Atlantic run until 1873 when switched to the Mediterranean. Sold to an Italian line in 1898 and scrapped the next year.

Taurus

Gross tonnage 1,126
Dimensions - m 64.1 x 9.0
Builder William Deny & Bros, Dumbarton
Maiden voyage 1853
Career Although built for the Mediterranean, served the Liverpool-New York route before being requisitioned in 1854 for the Crimean War. Sold in 1859 to the Spanish Government.

Teneriffe

Gross tonnage 1,127
Dimensions - m 64.00 x 8.84
Builder William Denny & Bros, Dumbarton
Maiden voyage 1854
Career Sailed on the Mediterranean service. Sold in 1859 to the Spanish Government.

Transylvannia

Gross tonnage 14,315
Dimensions - m 167.3 x 20.3
Builder Scott's of Greenock
Maiden voyage 1914
Career Built for the Anchor Line-Cunard partnership for the Mediterranean-New York run. Requisitioned as a troopship in 1915. Torpedoed in 1917 in the Gulf of Genoa while fully loaded and sunk with the loss of 414 lives.

Tripoli

Gross tonnage 2,057
Dimensions - m 89.2 x 11.6
Builder J & G Thomson, Glasgow
Maiden voyage 1865
Career Built for the Cunard Mediterranean service but sailed mainly on the Liverpool-New York route. Wrecked on the Tuskar Rocks south of Ireland on her 50th voyage with no loss of life.

Tuscania

Gross tonnage 14,348
Dimensions - m 167.4 x 20.3
Builder Alexander Stephen & Sons, Glasgow
Maiden voyage 1915
Career Sailed for the Cunard-Anchor Line partnership. In 1915 rescued 400 people from the blazing Greek ship Athenai. Requisitioned as a troop carrier in 1916 and made three Atlantic crossings before being torpedoed off Ireland in 1918 with the loss of 230 lives.

Tuscania II

Gross tonnage 16,991
Dimensions - m 181.97 x 21.34
Builder Fairfield Shipbuilding, Glasgow
Maiden voyage 1926
Career Built for Anchor Line in 1922 and acquired
by Cunard in 1926. Chartered in 1930 and sold
to a Greek Line in 1939. Returned to Cunard
management when requisitioned as troop carrier
during WW2. Scrapped in 1959.

Ultonia

Gross tonnage 8,845
Dimensions - m 152.4 x 17.5
Builder Swan Hunter, Newcastle
Maiden voyage 1898
Career Built as a cattle boat but converted for the
emigrant trade in 1904 sailing from Trieste to New
York. Carried troops in 1914, but returned to Cunard
service before being sunk by a U-boat off Land's End
in 1917.

Umbria

Gross tonnage 7,718
Dimensions - m 152.9 x 17.4
Builder John Elder & Co, Glasgow
Maiden voyage 1884
Career With the Eturia, the last Cunarder to be built
with sails. Served the Atlantic run, although service
interrupted by requisitioning in 1885 and 1900 for the
Boer Wars, and by a broken propeller shaft in 1892.
Scrapped in 1910.

Vauban

Gross tonnage 10,660
Dimensions - m 151.0 x 18.5
Builder Workman, Clark & Co, Belfast
Maiden voyage 1919
Career Built in 1912 for the Lampord & Holt line for
the River Plate Service. Chartered by Cunard 1919-22
for the Liverpool-New York run. Scrapped in 1932.